TEEN INVESTING COMPLETE GUIDE

A Beginner-Friendly Introduction to Stocks, ETFs, Bonds, and Long-Term Investing Basics

Ryan Bitstone

ISBN: 9781807651060

Published by TPSA Publishing

Introduction

The benefits of investing early on are enormous: You can get started much sooner than if you start at age 20, at which point many 401(k) accounts locked up until retirement. You'll be able to choose from different investments that grow at different rates so you can try out what fits with your goals. And you'll be able to give your money a head start on the decades ahead.

There are so many reasons to start investing now, not least of all because the stock market has historically returned an average annual rate of 9%. However, if you wait until you're older, other factors come into play. For example, by starting now, you'll have more time to ride out ups and downs and get over your fears of the unknown. When you're young, it's easier to recover from financial setbacks because your personal economy isn't as developed as that of an older investor's. You also can stash away extra money without having to cut back on spending in other areas. And if you invest while you're still in high school, you could get a head start on your retirement and college funds.

Another advantage of investing early is that if you hold on to the investment for many years and decades, your earnings will compound to volumes unachievable if you invest later in life. It's like compounding interest—money reinvested earns money on top of itself—but for stocks. So if you invest $5,000 at age 20 (assuming a 9% return), it will be worth about $131,000 when you're 65.

According to the U.S. Securities and Exchange Commission, "*You learn a lot in the first 20 years of your life. You learn how to eat and sleep, walk and talk about politics, deal with friends, teachers, bosses and coworkers. But there is one thing you don't do a lot of while you are young: Invest.*"Sadly, that's what most teens do: not invest. According to a UBS/Gallup Investor and Retirement Optimism report published on May 2nd in The Washington Post, only 14% of teenagers (ages 13-19) have invested in stocks or stock mutual funds. In comparison, 18% of adults age 30 and older have done so.

What's worse is that most teenagers don't even open a savings account or put money into other long-term investments. According to the UBS/Gallup report, only 40% of 13-19-year-olds have ever opened a savings account, and only 6% have put money into stocks or stock mutual funds. But when you hit your 20s, it's too late to start investing for retirement (at least through a company like Vanguard). *"There are many reasons young people are not investing in the stock market,"* said Kirk Chisholm of Chisholm Financial Group LLC in McLean, Virginia. *"Some are afraid of losing money; some don't know how much they need to save to reach a particular goal; and some are confused about the right investment vehicles."*

But by investing now, you can learn the ropes of the market before you need your money for retirement. "It's never too early to begin planning your financial future," *said Chisholm*. "The sooner that starts, and the more resources invested, the better off you will be when it comes time to use those resources."

You also have plenty of time to invest in different ways and try new investment strategies. Continue reading to know more!

CHAPTER 1. 10 REASONS TO START

To fabricate riches, you ought to invest your cash. On the off chance that you don't invest, you will pass up freedoms to build your monetary worth. Obviously, you can possibly lose cash in investments, however in the event that you invest carefully, the possibility to acquire is higher. If not invested, the purchasing influence of your cash will devalue extra time. Top reasons why you ought to invest your cash are:

1. **Abundance Creation** — Investing your cash will permit it to develop. Most investment vehicles, for example, stocks, testaments of store, or securities, offer profits for your cash over long haul. This return permits your cash to compound, bringing in cash on target previously procured and making abundance over the long haul.

2. **Beat Inflation** — 100 rupees today would just be 96.5 rupees one year from now as per late Indian expansion measurements, which infers that you would lose 4.5% of our cash each year whenever kept as money. Gets back from the investment keeps up the buying power at a consistent level. In the event that you don't beat the swelling rate you'd lose cash, not bringing in cash.

3. **Retirement corpus creation** — An individual ought to invest while he is procuring in order to make a corpus of assets that can be utilized when one resigns. This retirement store gathers extra time and gives security to keep an agreeable way of life even after retirement.

4. **Achieve monetary objectives** — Investing can help you arrive at greater monetary objectives. This profit for your investments can be utilized toward major monetary objectives, for example, purchasing a home, purchasing a vehicle, going into business, or setting up your kids for school.

5. **Duty saving** — Some investment vehicles give a twofold return by giving returns just as lessening your available pay, which thusly limits the expense obligation, for example, value

connected reserve funds plot (ELSS) reserves. Cash set aside is cash acquired which can be invested further.

6. **Significant yields** — Investing would assist with accomplishing exceptional yields when contrasted with bank's saving record, which gives a simple 4% return. Investing in business sectors could give you returns as much as 20% whenever given the opportune time skyline.

Actuality: If an individual invested Rs 724 in June 1989, then the sum would have compounded to Rs 34,903 today!

Prior to pushing forward, an investor needs to comprehend the idea of danger return compromise.

Danger Return Compromise

Regardless of whether you are making an investment in value in the securities exchange, land, government bonds or some other monetary instrument, there are these two factors your investment is ensured to have: danger and return. Simply, hazard alludes to the likelihood of bringing about misfortunes comparative with your investment. No investment exists that is totally hazard-free. Return gauges the genuine addition or misfortune your investment creates. While the word return is most regularly connected with an addition, it is completely conceivable to have a negative return, clearly showing a genuine misfortune on your investment. The danger/return tradeoff is consequently an investment rule that demonstrates a connected connection between these two investment factors.

The tradeoff is very basic: investments with higher danger are related to a more prominent likelihood of better yield, while investments with lower hazard have a more noteworthy likelihood of more modest return.

Youthful investors ought to have high extent of value in their portfolio as their danger-taking limit is more. More established individuals who are near their retirement age ought not to invest in value yet should search for fixed pay instruments, for example, bonds, debentures and government protections as they would give a constant flow of incomes with least conceivable danger.

Sorts of Investment Choices Accessible

1. **Value** — Stock investments address value proprietorship in a traded on an open market organization. Organizations issue stock as a component of a capital-raising system that subsidizes the activities of the organization. Corporate shares have shifting development prospects and are commonly dissected dependent on attributes, for example, assessed future profit and cost-to-income proportions. Stocks can be ordered in different classifications. Stocks may likewise offer profits adding a pay payout segment to the investment.

2. **Fixed Income Instruments** —Bonds are perhaps the most notable fixed pay items. They can be offered by governments or organizations. They are likewise given as a feature of an organization's capital-raising system. Bonds pay investors premium as coupon installments and offer full head reimbursement at development. Securities are ordinarily evaluated by a FICO assessment office, which offers understanding of their capital construction and capacity to make opportune installments.

3. **Favored Shares** — are ideal option for hazard opposed value investors in light of the fact that these are portions of an organization's stock with profits that are paid out to investors, before regular stock profits are given.

4. **Common Funds** — are comprised of a pool of assets gathered from numerous investors to invest in protections, for example, stocks, securities, currency market instruments and comparable resources. Shared assets are worked by cash directors who invest the asset's capital and endeavor to deliver capital additions and pay for the asset's investors.

5. **Subsidiaries** — Derivatives are investment items that are offered dependent on the development of a predetermined fundamental resource. Put or call choices on stocks and fates dependent on the development of items costs are the most widely recognized type of subordinate investment.

CHAPTER 2. HOW TO EARN YOUR OWN MONEY AND INCREASE YOUR GOALS-BUDGET

So, you're sixteen or older and you still live with your parents. Maybe you do a bit of work around the house like cleaning or doing the dishes, but don't feel like you can make your voice heard when it comes to what food should be on the dinner table tonight. Or maybe your parents are just not interested in meeting your needs.

The good news is that there are many ways for teenagers to have some fun and earn their own money. Here's how:

- **Pocket Money.** Ask for a small weekly allowance at home by giving an example of the things they would pay for with their money (like books, movies, clothes). If parents are not in a position to give you any money, ask for something else (like spending money, lunch at the school, etc.).

- **Summer Jobs.** Work on your own after school. You can do volunteer work or babysit. Check out companies near your house that hire teenagers.

- **Get a "Real Job".** Try to be a supervisor for your favorite fast food place or supermarket, or get a job at a local mall.

- **Add Work Experience.** Ask around for part-time jobs you can do during the summer holidays or on vacations: busboy, salesman, pizza delivery boy, etc.

- **Work in the "Growth" Economy.** Advertise for a part-time job at your local business and ask if they can give you a ride there. If you're under eighteen, have your teacher or others call the business for you. Many businesses will hire teens, sign them up for work experience with no pay and then ask them to come back part-time when school reopens.

- **Start a Business.** You can start a business with your friends. You can invite your friends to help and be the boss. If you're under eighteen, check with the school or parents first because businesses will not hire teens unless they are old enough to be able to work legally and have a Social Security number.

- **Gifts from relatives.** You may find that some relatives will give you money for your birthday or Christmas. It could be a nice surprise to open up present and find some cash in the card envelope!

- **Summer Jobs.** Many people do part-time jobs during the summer. This is one of the most common ways for teens to make money. Many students work in gas stations or restaurants and can earn enough money to buy gifts for themselves and their friends.

- **Selling things that you no longer need**. You probably have many items around your house which are used but still have some value. If your parents aren't using an item, why not sell it at a yard sale? You could get some extra money from these items and donate some of it to charity (or spend it yourself!).

- **Babysitting.** Many parents ask their friends and relatives for recommendations of babysitters. Invite them over for dinner or ask them to meet you at an event and they will become more likely to give you their contact information or ask for yours. You can add this information to your own contacts and start babysitting when they're out of town. It's a simple way of making money, but can be very rewarding!

- **If you have an online presence, you could make money from advertising revenue.** Online advertisers often pay for advertising based on the amount of views or clicks your website receives from users who access it through links they place on their site.

CHAPTER 3. GETTING AND MANAGING MONEY

Where to Put Your Money

Most teens have part-time jobs, babysitting jobs, or allowance they earn from helping out around the house. That money needs to be put to work for teens' long-term future. They can't afford to just put the money in a piggy bank or under their mattress and forget about it. Here are some options parents should discuss with their teens before deciding what to do with their savings.

Savings Accounts

Savings accounts are the most commonplace for teens to save their money.

Many banks offer different types of savings accounts:

- Interest-bearing accounts may pay teens a little bit of interest (meaning they earn a small percentage of the amount in the account).

- No-fee accounts may earn the same interest as interest-bearing accounts, but they don't come with any fees.

- Online savings accounts can be more convenient than traditional bank branches, as you can transfer money quickly and pay bills online.

It's important to compare different options and make sure you understand what the fees are for each option so you can decide what's best for your family.

Checking Accounts

Another option is a checking account that offers savings features. It allows teens to have a checking account like adults but also earn interest on their money. While most checking accounts don't usually earn a lot of interest, there is a new type of checking account that does. It's called a high-yield checking account. With this type of account, teens can earn more interest than with traditional savings accounts and have the convenience of a checking account, including being able to make withdrawals and deposits at anytime and anywhere, using ATMs or bank branches.

Certificates of Deposit (CDs)

A certificate of deposit is similar to a savings account in that it generally offers higher interest rates than other investment options (though CDs are not usually as liquid). CDs require a certain amount of money to be deposited for periods ranging from one month up to five years. If the money is withdrawn before the end of the deposit period, it may result in a penalty.

Laws, Taxes and Tax-Friendly Investments: Tips for Parents

What are custodial accounts?

Custodial accounts are created for minors (children under 18). These accounts can be either set up by parents or grandparents and allow the child access to his money.

If a minor has earned income, such as delivering newspapers, babysitting or working part-time at McDonald's, that money can be deposited into his custodial account and used for whatever the child sees fit. Or it can be used to pay for an education.

Why would you want to set up a custodial account?

Perhaps the best reason is that you want to give your child a head start in learning about managing money. It is an excellent opportunity to both learn and practice a variety of financial skills, from saving to making investment decisions. Your child will learn that money is a finite, valuable resource that must be used wisely.

The custodial account provides a neat tax shelter as well. You can deposit up to $1,900 annually into the account on behalf of your child. That amount grows tax-deferred until it is withdrawn by your child when he reaches the age of majority (18 or 21 depending on state laws). To open a custodial savings account, the parent must open an individual account in his own name and fund it with $50 worth of U.S. series EE savings bonds. Or you can make a cash deposit into the account. You will then need to obtain a custodial savings certificate with the name of the child and file it with your state's office of securities. You can take advantage of all the same tax-advantaged accounts for your children as you do for yourself: IRAs, 401(k)s, SEPs, Keoghs and Profit-Sharing Plans. You can direct up to $1,900 annually to these accounts on behalf of your child. The money is taxed when it is taken out by the child at age 18 or 21 depending on state laws.

In some cases, it might be advantageous to set up these accounts in the child's name rather than the parent's. This would allow you to avoid "kiddie tax" on investment income over $1,900. If you expect your child to have investment income greater than that amount, it might be wise to explore this option with an accountant or financial planner.

What are UGMA and UTMA accounts?

These are Uniform Gifts to Minors Act and Uniform Transfers to Minors Act accounts, which allow parents or grandparents to make gifts of money or stock directly to a minor. Any income or growth is taxed in the hands of the minor as if he had earned it.

UGMA and UTMA accounts are useful where the parents or grandparents don't have much in the way of a taxable income. (You can make only one outright gift per year to an individual regardless of how many accounts he holds.) This is also an easy way for grandparents to provide assistance for grandchildren's higher education expenses without having to worry about annual gift tax limits.

Opening an UGMA or UTMA account is a very simple process. The deed or title of the assets must be transferred into the name of someone over 18 years old with "custodian" written in parenthesis next to his name. For example: Joe Blow, custodian for John Doe. The custodian can be either the parent or another adult that the child trusts (such as an aunt or uncle). A parent or caregiver must open an individual account in his name and deposit $50 worth of U.S. savings bonds into it. Then the assets —stocks, a bank account, etc. — are transferred to the individual account named in the deed of trust by your bank or broker.

UGMA and UTMA accounts are a great way to start teaching kids about money from a young age. They are particularly appropriate for children who have special needs or disabilities because they allow parents to help them with their financial affairs without going through a court procedure for guardianship. If the child turns 18 and uses all of the money, he can simply transfer any unused assets back into his own name or a new account.

When you set up UGMA or UTMA accounts for your children, it is important to include a brief letter with them explaining why you set up these accounts. A lawyer could draft such a letter for you if you wish. The purpose of including this letter with your offspring's securities is to alert the child, if she ever questions her holdings that someone loves and cares about her. It will also explain what is expected of her if and when it comes time to use these assets.

One possible scenario is that the child may need some money for an emergency and she is completely unprepared. If she doesn't understand the purpose of an UGMA or UTMA account, it could create a situation where she may misuse your assets. The letter can also provide a list of talking points to have with her if she chooses to discuss this issue with her friends or instructors.

For example, you might write:

"I've set aside some money for you as a way to help you through school. You can use it to finish your education or to start out in a career. I've written out a list of options for you. You will need to do some serious thinking and planning before you use any of it:

- Pay tuition for the rest of your undergraduate education
- Pay for graduate school
- Start a business
- Buy a car or home

If you choose to take some money out, please remember that this is on top of your regular income and expenses. Please see me and we can discuss how this might affect your other funds. Also keep in mind that the principal is what matters most and I hope you will think long term about how best to use it.

If you take some money out, please let me know how it helps so I can put it in your file".

IRAs

Joy is a hard worker. Although she didn't finish high school, she found a stable job. She worked as a warehouse manager for thirty long years. The pay is good, but she ended up spending all she got. When she finally retired, she only saved up $10,000, which only covers a few months of her living expenses. Her pension benefits are simply not enough.

Unfortunately, Joy's story is not unique. More and more retirees are broke.

To avoid ending up like Joy, it is best to invest in an IRA.

IRA or Individual Retirement Account is a tax-advantaged investment and a savings account that allows you to save for retirement.

There are different types of IRA, namely—traditional IRA, Roth IRA, Simple IRA, Spousal IRA, nondeductible IRA, SEP IRA, and self-directed IRA. You will be able to evaluate which seems to be more convenient according to your and your children's needs.

CHAPTER 4. BUSINESS AND FINANCIAL CONCEPTS

Net Worth

Net worth is the value of all of a person's assets subtracting the value of their liabilities. Assets are things such as cash, stocks, bonds, mutual funds, products held for sale in the business (inventory), real estate and other property. Liabilities are accounts payable such as mortgage payments and other debts.

Inflation

Inflation is a sustained increase in the general level of prices for goods and services, where the rate of price increase is higher than in previous periods. It is also a decrease in the purchasing power of money, which means that you need more money to buy a given product or service.

Liquidity

Liquidity is the degree to which an asset or security can be quickly bought or sold in the market without affecting the asset's price.

Bull Market

A buyer market alludes to a market that is on the ascent, which is something to be thankful for. That implies that costs of offers in the market are expanding. Generally, a positively trending market likewise implies the economy is in a decent state, and the degree of joblessness is low. The US is at present in a positively trending market.

Bear Market

A bear market is something contrary to bull. As such, the market is declining. Offer costs are diminishing, the economy is in a destruction, and joblessness levels are rising.

Risk Tolerance

Risk tolerance is a term used in investment, finance, and economics to describe the amount of uncertainty that an individual or an institution will be able to endure. A high-risk tolerance indicates that the individual or entity can handle volatile markets and maintain their investments during downturns.

Asset Allocation and Diversification

Asset allocation and diversification are two investment strategies that are used to minimize the risk of an investment portfolio. These strategies can be implemented in a number of ways but the common goal is to reduce overall portfolio volatility.

Interest

Interest is a cost incurred as the result of borrowing money from another individual or company. If you borrow $5,000, you may pay back $7,000 after four years. The difference between the two numbers (the original loan and what is owed) is your total interest that is more than doubled. A person might get an interest-free loan if they are living in poverty or have low credit and would otherwise find it difficult to secure a loan on their own.

Compound Interest

Compound interest is when interest earned on a deposit or loan accrues and compounds, so that the compounding occurs not only on the initial amount but also on past earnings (so that it "grows from itself"). This means that compound interest can cause the total to increase exponentially, rather than arithmetically.

Interest, or simple interest, is an aggregate you pay for having utilized a monetary assistance: for example, the interest you pay to the bank for a home loan or any loan specified.

As you most likely are aware, the longer the span of the loan, the more prominent the general interest you pay to the bank, in light of the fact that the last will take more time to gather the whole sum that has been progressed to you.

We should make a qualification quickly: simple or compound interest? Simple interest is the one characterized above, while compound interest will be interest on interest. We contextualize simple interest and compound interest both in the realm of monetary investments, which is the thing that interests us explicitly.

Simple interest is the return that is paid to you reliably, in light of an underlying invested capital, which doesn't increment since you intermittently pull out the profit.

I'll give you a solid model.

Invest an amount of $20,000 in an instrument with which you procure 10% per annum, you will get yourself an amount of $22,000 toward the year's end; in this way pull out the $2,000 of benefit and rehash a similar investment with the underlying capital consistently of $20,000. Following 10 years, you will get yourself $40,000, or you will have multiplied the underlying capital. Compound interest, then again, depends on the ceaseless reinvestment of the collected profit, without the withdrawal toward the year's end. Take a similar model again yet, in the wake of procuring $2,000 in the principal year, invest the total amassed capital in the subsequent year, for example the amount of $22,000 and not $20,000 as in the primary model.

The underlying invested capital will step by step increment after every year and subsequently the yearly profit will increment appropriately.

In this subsequent case, following 10 years you will procure $51,875.

In the picture underneath you can perceive what occurs in the two instances of simple interest and compound interest.

Do you comprehend the significance of compound interest and for what reason do you need to utilize it to acquire it over the long run? Disregard simple interest and from this point forward stress over taking advantage of compound interest in your investments.

The power of compounding interest is one of the most useful financial tools at one's disposal. First and foremost, it stresses the importance of saving money from early on to maximize the total amount obtained later in life. Secondly, it uses compound interest to reach the ambitious goal of amassing $500,000.00 by the time one's life is over. Thirdly, it emphasizes that not only does one need a lot of money saved up but also must follow the advised system of putting aside money without interruption. If one quits saving after just five years then they will have accumulated less than $100,000.00! The power of compounding interest is powerful but not every investment plan can survive in its wake. It is important to avoid risky investments and to stick with those that are more stable like bonds and savings accounts that traditionally have higher interest rates than other types of investments.

How Market Works

The first question you probably have is what causes these fluctuations in the first place. The answer is a little more complex than most people think. It is true that there are many factors that can cause market changes, but they're a response to changes in consumer demand, which is actually caused by inflation and unemployment rates. Yes, it's about supply and demand; we all know about this concept, right? Rest assured, these concepts aren't just complicated for complicatedness' sake! Instead, they help you understand how market movements occur and how you can use them to your advantage when trading or investing.

When you go out and purchase something, you're creating demand. You put money into the economy, and that money goes into someone else's pocket. That person then uses it to buy a candy bar or a new pair of shoes, and then he or she might spend that money on beer or cigarettes. This endless cycle eventually creates inflation. What does this have to do with markets? Well, when you see market shifts, they're usually triggered by changes in inflation or unemployment rates. Investors will sell their stocks or bonds if they are worried that inflation is going to rise and may make those investments worthless.

Unemployment and inflation rates are caused by various factors, such as technological advances or the global economy, which means that you can't predict them from looking at the news. However, one thing is certain: if these rates change drastically in a short period of time, investors will sell their stocks because of the possibility of more inflation. You might be wondering how a change in unemployment rates would create a change in market behavior, but this is actually very straightforward if you understand how governments usually deal with these problems. When an economy suffers from high levels of unemployment, the government will often engage in expansionary fiscal policy, which means they are borrowing money to stimulate spending. As a result of borrowing money, interest rates will fall because there's more cash chasing after bonds; this can stimulate more spending and economic activity. In response to this, inflation will rise a bit. Once the economy is stimulated, investors feel more comfortable investing their money in those companies that are doing well.

CHAPTER 5. THE RIGHT TIME AND THE RIGHT WAY TO INVEST

Investing is not a game, and it's time to start playing by the rules. You need to understand the risks, find the right environment, and manage your allocation. If you've ever talked about investing with someone who has made a lot of money in business or on Wall Street, odds are they have a wealth management team backing them up who takes care of all this complicated stuff for them. But what if you do it? In order for investing to work for you, you need to educate yourself before making any decisions about where your money should go. The investment world will capitalize on your ignorance, and you'll lose money. So, where do you start?

How about with the right time and the right way?

First, there's the right time. What do I mean by this? Investing is not a get-rich-quick scheme. It's a slow, steady process that can take years to really pay off — if it pays off at all. Don't be in a hurry to reach your goals; that will just put undue stress on you. Take your time and do it right.

Next, there's the right way. The right way to invest is to follow the rules—and not your emotions. If you are thinking of buying a stock, ask yourself why you want to buy it. Is it because you have done a lot of homework and know the company or is it just because the stock price has gone up (and who doesn't want that)? The answer is probably the latter. The best investors spend 80% of their time doing research and 20% doing everything else—such as buying stocks—and they don't buy anything until they are prepared to do so because they are looking at what's happening with the company. Buying on emotion is how people lose money, and it's exactly what most investors do. Don't let this be you.

Investing is a scary word for many because it seems so daunting. With people living longer, the need to put away money for your retirement is more pressing than ever. That's where we come in!

Here are five easy steps on how to invest in the right way, so you can sleep well at night knowing that your finances are safe and sound:

1) Educate yourself about investing and take some time to thoroughly consider what you want from your investment account. Knowing what kind of investment product will work best for you will allow for making a better decision when it comes time to invest as there won't be as many unknowns about possible outcomes of investments or potential risks involved with these potential investments.

2) Once you have a better understanding of the different types of investments available, it's time to compare the costs. This includes analyzing what it will cost on an annual basis to maintain the investment and any other possible fees that may be associated with the investment product as a whole.

3) Calculate your goals and figure out how much you need for your savings. Depending on your budget, determine whether or not you can afford to save a certain amount each month to reach this goal. If your budget doesn't allow for monthly contributions, you can still start saving by making one lump sum payment every so often (e.g.: 3 or 4 times a year).

4) Always do your research on potential investments to be sure that they meet your criteria and needs. As with anything else, knowledge is power.

5) Once you have chosen which investment will work best for you, it's time to get started! Remember that the sooner you invest, the greater your returns will be over the long term. If however, you have many immediate concerns (mortgage payments or college tuition), make sure to invest what is most important first and then build up from there.

What Are SMART Goals?

SMART is an acronym that describes a goal-setting formula that has been proven to be highly effective in helping people achieve their goals.

The acronym stands for:

- **S**pecific: Try to be clear and specific with what you want. The narrower your goal, the more you'll understand the steps necessary to reach it.

- **M**easurable: Set measurable milestones along your way will give you the opportunity to evaluate or correct your steps. When you achieve your milestones, always remember to reward yourself even in small ways.

- **A**ttainable: Setting goals you can reasonably achieve within a certain timeframe will help keep you motivated and focused.

- **R**elevant: Each of your goals should align with your values and larger, long-term goals.

- **T**ime-specific: An end-date will help you prioritize and can provide motivation.

By adhering to these standards, you can make sure that whatever financial goals you set for yourself will be achievable. Once you have set your goals, it is important that you take action immediately to keep them from being forgotten.

How Does Setting SMART Financial Goals Help Me Achieve Success?

The key element of SMART goal-setting is specificity. If you set a goal that is too broad, it will be hard to measure whether you have achieved it. For example, if your goal is to save up money for a down payment for a house, that may be very difficult to achieve unless you set the date of when you plan on buying your house. By setting specific financial goals and deadlines, it will be much easier to monitor your progress. You will also find that other elements of SMART goal-setting will help you achieve financial success. By keeping track of your goals and keeping them relevant to your life and needs, you can make sure they are attainable, and by making them time-specific, you make sure that they are something which must be completed in a timely manner.

How Do I Set the Best Financial Goals?

First, you must decide what your goal is. There are many ways in which people can set financial goals. If you are saving a lot of money, you may want to set a goal for how much you want to save by the end of each month. If you are trying to pay off debt, it may be best to focus on how much debt you can pay off by the end of each month or how much interest and principal payments will be made towards a specific debt at the end of three months. If your goal is ultimately to save up for retirement, 3–5 years would be a good timeframe in which to work towards that goal. By thinking about what your goals are, you can determine whether it is worth the time and effort to set a specific goal or if you should just be saving what you can.

CHAPTER 6. UNDERSTANDING AND INVESTING IN BONDS

If you have an investment portfolio, there's a good chance that some of your holdings are in bonds. But if you're not sure what bonds are, how they work, or how you can learn more about them, don't worry! We'll answer the most common questions and get you up to speed with this basic introduction to understanding and investing in bonds.

What Is a Bond?

A bond is basically like getting an IOU from the government (or another entity). The entity creates a document stating that it owes someone X dollars on Y date. When the entity pays back what it owes at maturity date (which could be any time over 20 years), it pays back with interest.

What is the government selling bonds for?

The government's main reason for selling bonds is to raise money for various projects. They sell bonds at a set rate of interest to investors, who receive periodic interest payments and then get paid back with the principal when the bond matures.

When Is the Government Going to Start Paying Back What It Owes?

The government usually sells bonds with a maturity of 10 years or less. Of course, that means that if you buy a 30-year bond, you'll be getting your principal back when you're in your 50s.

How Do I Know that the Government Is Really Going to Pay Me Back?

You can think of bonds as similar to what happens when you buy a house. The bank will lend you the money, but it will use your house as collateral. If you don't pay the money back, the bank can foreclose and take your house. Similarly, if a country doesn't pay its bondholders back, or only pays them back with another bond (called a "debt swap"), there are consequences. Because bonds are traded on exchanges (like stocks), their value changes based on supply and demand and interest rates. If a government makes bondholders wait too long to get their principal back, they can ask the government for a lower interest rate. This means that the government will pay less interest, and that is one way that it can be forced to pay back its debt at a faster rate.

How Does This Affect Me?

If you buy a bond (and there are many different kinds of bonds), you would collect interest on your investment from the entity that owes you money. You'll get paid at regular intervals (every 6 months in the case of US treasury bonds), and when the bond matures, you would get back your principal (again, this could be ten years in the future).

How Do I Buy a Bond?

If you'd like to be an investor in bonds, you need to do two things. First, you need to decide which country or entity you want to be invested in. This is called making a "country allocation". In the US, bonds can be bought at your local bank or at any brokerage. They can also be traded on exchanges like stocks (for example, you could buy IBM bonds and sell Apple bonds). Bonds pay interest every 6 months (or other regularly occurring intervals).

What Are My Options for Investing in Bonds?

There are many different kinds of bonds with different payouts and risks associated with them. Depending on your goals and risk tolerance, you might want to choose different types of bonds. US Treasury Bonds (often called T-Bonds) are considered very low risk. They have a "AAA" rating and are backed by the US government. This means that if the entity that owes you money (the US government) falls behind in payment, the US will step in to pay its bondholders. T-bonds are easy, safe investments but pay low-interest rates. Corporate bonds (corporate IOUs) have a lower risk than T-bonds because corporations will not be bailed out by the government if they fall behind on their payments. However, their risk is still higher than T-bonds. Their interest rates are higher as well. Municipal bonds are issued by state and local governments, and they're considered to have the lowest risk of default of any bonds because the entities that issue them can always raise taxes if they need more money. They pay lower interest rates than corporate bonds but higher interest rates than T-bonds. As you can see, there are many different kinds of bonds, with a wide range of risks and potential returns associated with each kind of bond. Luckily, there are financial advisors that can help you sort through the options available to find ones that work for you and your goals.

Government Bonds

Bonds issued by the federal government are called government bonds and are considered to be risk-free investments. Unlike corporate bonds, government bonds don't have any credit risk attached to them because you know that the issuer is guaranteed by the federal government. Bonds issued by corporations, on the other hand, can default and usually do so without any warning! Because of this higher credit risk, corporate bonds offer a higher yield than their safer counterparts.

Corporate Bonds

Corporate bonds are debt securities issued by companies (rather than governments) to borrow money from investors at a future date with an agreement to pay out at least some interest over time and then repay the principal amount borrowed at maturity. The borrower pays the lender an interest rate that is set at the time of issuance based on the creditworthiness of the company. The riskier the company, or lower its credit rating, the higher (or "riskier") a yield you can expect from buying that company's bonds.

Corporate bonds are generally much more volatile in value than government bonds due to their higher risk, however they offer higher yields as well.

Corporate Bonds also trade actively on what's known as the "secondary market" while Government Bonds are traded mostly on what's known as the "primary market". The most common way to purchase bonds is through brokerage accounts. There are a number of large brokerages which cater to individual investors, making it easy to place trades for as little as a few hundred dollars. Some brokerages even have minimums as low as $1 for bond trades.The other way to invest in bonds is through mutual funds that invest in corporate and government bonds. Investors can buy into these funds with just a few hundred dollars. The fees associated with mutual funds, however, take away from any returns on your investment in the fund. These fees can eat away at the gains you make on the investment and may even make it unprofitable in some cases.

There are many types of bonds (corporate, government) that may be worth considering for investment. For example, US Savings Bonds are issued by the US Treasury. These bonds pay a fixed interest rate every six months until they mature 30 years from the issue date. Some Savings Bonds may be cashed in before maturity, but at a steep loss as compared to what could have been earned had the full term been held to maturity.

Corporate bonds come in many different types of ratings and price points. High-quality corporate bonds that carry high credit ratings from Standard & Poor's or Moody's are usually considered to be safer than lower-credit rated corporate bonds. The lower the credit rating, also known as the corporate bond's "credit spread," the higher the yield an investor may expect to receive. The greater the risk, however, is usually accompanied by a greater expected return. High-risk bonds (i.e. junk bonds) can pay double-digit yields but also have a high likelihood of default.

This is the perfect time to learn about bonds—because know-how could save you a boat load of money! Read on to find out when it makes sense, and when it doesn't, to invest in bonds. Bonds are for more than just old people: they can be used strategically by young people too. They provide a tax benefit and can be a good way to diversify your portfolio. But before you buy any bonds, there are some things you need to know. Bonds are not all the same—there is a difference between "securities" and "obligations," with securities being riskier than obligations. Plus there are short-term bonds and long-term bonds, and how you choose to use these will affect your return.

Since bonds do not have the same liquidity as stocks, you need to know when is a good time to buy them —and when it's not. You also need to have an understanding of how bond prices are determined— and this understanding can only come from practice and experience. Most importantly, you must learn the basics of portfolio construction so that you can determine the appropriate mix of stocks and bonds for yourself. This means learning about risk assessment, asset allocation, diversification, and more. The market value of a bond depends on several factors: the maturity, the coupon rate, and most importantly—the credit rating. Yield to maturity determines the approximate price at which a security will trade in the open market. Also called interest-rate characteristics, yield to maturity tells us how much interest investors will receive before the bonds reach full maturity date. The more risk you are willing to take, the higher the bond yield will be.

The price of a bond is determined by its coupon rate and the yield to maturity. The price of a bond goes up as its yield goes down (or conversely, as its price goes up as its yield goes down). Trading volume and volatility also affect the bond's price. If there is any uncertainty about the payment of interest or principal amount at maturity, then bonds are less likely to be traded for their full value. This uncertainty usually results from a lower rating or from a high degree of financial leverage in the issuing firm (i.e., after-tax profit less total interest expense divided by gross debt equals 5%). The value of a bond increases when its duration is reduced.

A bond's maturity date determines the length of time that you are investing in the debt obligations of an entity. Bonds have a place in every portfolio, given that they offer tax advantages and interest income. When bonds are used as a short-term financial instrument, then they should seek capital gains and return on investment (ROI). Bonds are also used as part of the asset allocation process among investors; however, this type of strategy can lead to losses if the investor is not knowledgeable about these instruments. Bonds are also used as a longer-term investment and are particularly useful as a way to diversify one's portfolio. This kind of bond is used when an investor is concerned about the liquidity of the stock market. These bonds move in the opposite direction of stocks and provide an investor with an additional form of diversification. When short-term interest rates increase, then long-term interest rates usually increase correspondingly. Bond prices and yields move inversely to one another given that bonds are traded through yield.

CHAPTER 7. UNDERSTANDING AND INVESTING IN STOCKS

Stocks are a type of financial instrument, and when you invest in them, you're buying shares of ownership in a company. You may not have heard of many of the companies we'll talk about here, but they employ thousands of people and make products that you consume every day. In fact, it's possible that the companies on our list are even part of your portfolio already!

When you buy a share or stock in a company, there are two things at work: company earnings or profits, and the value (or price) that the market places on these profits. What are earnings? Well, they're simply what the company makes selling its products—think about how much profit any store owner makes by selling shoes. This is company earnings.

Now, the other factor involved in buying a stock is what the market will pay for these profits. What does that mean? When you buy a stock, you are effectively agreeing to pay a certain price for the portion of ownership that you are purchasing. The market dictates how much your stock is worth based on how profitable that company is and how much investors think its profits will increase (or decrease) in the future. Today, we'll focus on earning potential and growth so that we can better understand how you make money with stocks.

We'll also discuss the ways to invest in stocks. It's important to understand that you're not always going to buy a full share of stock, but rather a small percentage. In fact, most stocks are broken down into two or more shares for every one sold!

You've probably heard of people "diversifying" their portfolios. This means that rather than putting all of your eggs in one basket—or investing in just one type of stock—you're spreading out your money. When you diversify, you are offering yourself options so that if the company whose stock you bought has a rough quarter (or year), your portfolio won't become immediately worthless. To diversify, invest in stocks from a variety of companies in different sectors.

If you're looking to invest directly with the company, it's often a good idea to search for its financial information in advance so that you know exactly how much your investment is worth. You'll also need to decide whether or not you want your shares in common, preferred or limited form.

Here are the differences:

- **Common Stock**: This is the most traditional type of stock and it's generally worth more when the company is doing well. Many professional investors prefer to buy this stock because it's liquid (i.e., easy to sell and usually not restricted in any way).

- **Preferred Stock:** This is debt that the company owes you, but with a couple of big exceptions. The company isn't legally obligated to pay your dividends until they have paid off their debt, so your money is at risk until that time comes. Also, when the company goes bankrupt, you will be paid before those with common stock—but after those with bonds or preferred debt.

- **Limited Stock:** This is a hybrid between preferred and common stocks, as it offers some of the benefits of both while keeping some of the risks (and potential rewards) associated with each type. There is much less of this type of stock available than the other two, but it can be a good choice if you like the company and want to invest in its future.

When should you be buying stocks? And when should you be selling them? These are questions most investors ask themselves at some point in their investing careers. You'll often hear people say that timing the market is impossible, but that's not true. There are certain times of the year when stocks perform better than others, and there are many reasons why this is so. In this article I'm going to answer the question "when to buy and sell stocks".

If you're a value investor, you look for stocks with a low price/book value ratio and/or a low price/earnings ratio. These are the kind of companies that usually outperform the general market. But simply buying these stocks doesn't guarantee you'll make money. When you buy a stock your return is directly related to how much money is made by the company. This in turn depends on when is the right time of year to buy stocks.

Stock prices fluctuate throughout the year, but it's not random. Stock markets tend to perform better during specific periods of the year, and this has been proven by numerous studies over many years around the world. For example, stocks in the United States tend to perform better from October through April. This is known as the October Effect. The reason for this is that people look to rebalance their portfolios in December after all their summer spending, and they like to buy stocks when there's more money in the market. That means demand is high for stocks which improve their price performance.

But here's the real question... Is it worth doing? Some people say that timing the market is worth the effort while others argue it's a waste of time. I say it depends on your investment style. If you're a value investor, then I recommend looking at historical stock trends and trying to time your buying accordingly. After all, if you can get better performance without much risk with very little work, then why not? This way of investing is called passive investing and has been around for a long time. It's the basis of many investment strategies like dollar-cost averaging. It's also very simple and easy to understand, which is why so many people use it even though so few people actually succeed.

When Not to Buy Stocks

If you're not a value investor, then timing your stock purchases is probably a waste of time. If the prices are high, don't buy the stocks because you think they'll go even higher. Buying high and selling low isn't smart investing. It's gambling and the odds are against you. Don't try to time the market by buying at the lowest prices because that seldom works out well either unless you know what you're doing and have an edge in trading like day traders do. When in doubt, the middle ground is always the best choice. That's the way the average investor should play it, because if you're not a value investor and you try to time your stock purchases too much, then you're likely to lose money rather than gain it.

Additionally, On the off chance that you invested $1,000 in Amazon or Apple 10 years prior, that investment would have truly paid off. As per individual budget site DQYDJ, an underlying $1,000 investment in those organizations in 2008 would be valued at $16,239 and $8,587, separately, as of January 16. On the off chance that you invested $1,000 in Google in a similar time span, it would have paid off, as well. As indicated by DQYDJ, GOOGL would be valued at $3,660 as of January 16 and GOOG would be valued at $2,008. (Google's stock split into two classes in 2014: GOOGL: Alphabet Class An and GOOG: Alphabet Class C.) All things considered, the information shows that one company altogether beat Amazon, Apple and either class of Alphabet: Netflix. As of January 16, a $1,000 investment in the video-web-based feature would merit an incredible $70,263.

Netflix first dispatched its real-time feature in 2007, started delivering unique substance in 2013 and has developed its endorser base to almost 120 million records around the world. The company likewise added in excess of 8,000,000 supporters in the final quarter, CNBC reports, fundamentally more than Wall Street assumptions, and its shares have bounced in excess of 8%, bringing its market capitalization above $100 billion interestingly.

The company intends to burn through $7.5–8 billion on substance in 2018, including shows from titan Shonda Rhimes and comic book company Millarworld. *"We accept our enormous investments* in *substance are paying off,"* the company wrote in a letter to shareholders.

Be that as it may, while Netflix's stock has performed well and the company has high expectations for the future, any individual stock can over—or fail to meet expectations. Past returns don't foresee future outcomes.

Furthermore, there are a few difficulties not too far off. Contenders, like Disney, which has consented to purchase 21st Century Fox resources, might actually pull watchers from Netflix with plans to dispatch their own web-based features.

Disney's arrangement with Fox would give the consolidated company a stake in Netflix's adversary, Hulu. Furthermore, Amazon, Apple, Facebook and YouTube have added more substance to their separate stages.

So a few investors are bearish— Jim Cramer, host of CNBC's "Frantic Money," however, isn't one of them. With Netflix raising the month-to-month cost for its web-based feature and adding more unique substance to supplement effectively well-known shows like *"The Crown"* and *"More unusual Things,"* Cramer, in October, said the company could quicken its development significantly further.

Ted Sarandos, Netflix's main substance official, said he would not like to get "excessively diverted by *the* serious scene". *The company concurs*. "The market for amusement time is tremendous and can uphold numerous administrations", *it notes.* "Amusement administrations are regularly corresponding, given their extraordinary substance contributions. We accept this is to a great extent why both we and Hulu have had the option to succeed and develop."

In case you are thinking about getting into the stock market, specialists prompt start cautiously.

Experienced investors Warren Buffett, Mark Cuban and Tony Robbins propose you start with list reserves, which offer low turnover rates, specialist expenses and assessment charges, and vary with the market to take out the danger of picking singular stocks. DQYDJ's stock return mini-computer device, which accumulates its numbers from information stage Quandl, appropriately represents stock parts and special dividends by making an "information structure [that] contains the underlying buy and the value vacillations utilizing stock shutting costs every day," as per the site. "Typical parts and dividend occasions cause us to expand the displayed number of shares held. Invert parts will decrease the quantity of shares held." The outcomes are reserved for as long as multi-week so as not to overpower the information supplier. The adding machine doesn't account stock side projects. And keeping in mind that it has a reinvestment device, Netflix's end number, above, doesn't represent reinvestments.

CHAPTER 8. INDEX AND MUTUAL FUNDS: WHY NOT?

An index fund is a group of securities that track the performance of an index. A mutual fund is a professionally managed investment company that pools money from many investors and invests it according to a specific strategy, objective or theme.

A mutual fund may invest in stocks, bonds, money market securities and other investments. An index fund generally tries to match the performance of its benchmark indexes such as the S&P 500 Index or Wilshire 5000 Index which means investing in all stocks in these indices to replicate their composition and return. By investing in all the companies within the index, an index fund takes advantage of diversification which reduces risk and increases return.

Both mutual funds and index funds are managed investment vehicles. Both types of funds offer investors a convenient way to pool their money for investing in securities. Mutual funds have professional management while index funds typically do not. Mutual funds are subject to regulatory oversight and must file annual reports with the SEC, provide semi-annual reports to shareholders, file periodic shareholder reports with the SEC, provide audited financial statements every year and more. Mutual fund shares can only be purchased through a financial professional or an online broker. Index funds can be purchased directly from the fund sponsor without an intermediary, paying a commission.

Both mutual funds and index funds are available as "open-end" investment companies or "closed-end" investment companies. Open-end investment companies add to their capital by continually offering shares to the public for purchase.

Both mutual funds and index funds provide investors with diversification by investing in hundreds or thousands of securities within their respective indices or asset categories. A mutual fund may offer exposure to securities from all over the world or in specific areas such as technology, healthcare, energy and more. An index fund typically does not have the ability to invest in securities outside of its specific index. This limits the risks and rewards experienced by investors. Mutual funds and index funds are both very tax efficient. Both types of investments may generate capital gains when securities held within the fund are sold for a profit. Both types of funds can benefit from lower taxes by holding their investments within tax-advantaged accounts while waiting to sell other holdings or when redeeming shares into cash (see Taxes on Mutual Funds).

No-load mutual funds do not charge an up-front commission when shares are purchased directly from the fund company or through an online broker (see No-load Fund). Some mutual funds charge a deferred sales charge if shares are redeemed within a certain period after the purchase date (see Load Fund).

Both open-end mutual funds and closed-end index funds can be traded on an exchange at any time. Index funds within the same group (e.g., Vanguard 500 Index Fund, Vanguard Mid-Cap Index Fund) may be bought and sold at any time even though they have different net asset values (NAVs). Most mutual fund families allocate shares to investors on a pro-rata basis each day based on the investor's account balance.

The number of index funds available is much larger than the number available for mutual funds. In addition to specialized indexes such as an international index or a small-cap index there are more general-purpose broad market indexes such as the Russell 2000, S&P 500, Wilshire 5000 and Dow Jones Industrial Average. All of these indexes are tracked by corresponding mutual funds. The size and scope of these indices continually change and it is not uncommon for several new index funds to be launched while other existing index funds are closed or merged with other related index funds.

In theory, stock and bond market exchange prices can move faster than an individual investor's ability to execute transactions over multiple security types within a portfolio. For instance, an investor may wish to sell some bonds and purchase more stocks based upon a change in market conditions. With a mutual fund, investors can accomplish this by selling the bonds and buying the new stocks with a single transaction rather than selling one security then purchasing another separately. The individual investor can use an index fund alone or in combination with other investment strategies such as stock investing, bond investing and money market investing. Index Fund Investing is the practice of utilizing index funds to build a diversified portfolio of securities for investment purposes.

Because no active (human) decision-making is involved in maintaining the portfolio, costs are low relative to actively managed funds. Actively managed funds depend on a manager to make buying and selling decisions in an attempt to outperform their chosen benchmark index. This can be costly, as the fund manager receives a percentage of asset under management each year. For example, an actively managed fund might charge a 1.5% annual management fee whereas an index fund may charge close to or less than .20%, and some indices like the S&P 500 are even free to invest in passively. In addition, there is still the cost of trading which will come out of your pocket every time you buy or sell a security in your portfolio. Another cost associated with actively managed mutual funds is the Bid-ask spread. This is the amount of money it costs to get in and out of a position quickly. An index fund has no management to make buying or selling decisions so there aren't any trading costs associated. The Bid-ask spread varies across investment products and markets, but an average study found that this spread averaged between 1/2% to 1% per trade, meaning it costs more to trade with an actively managed mutual fund than an index fund. An index fund investor doesn't have to worry about what the stock market will do; the indices or indexes they're investing in are designed to track the overall performance of an index like the S&P 500 or various sectors of the economy. The investor also doesn't have to worry about picking stocks or companies that may be losing money. The value of an index fund's investment is based on the value of all the holdings in that index, so if a company loses money, it won't affect your portfolio's performance. If you have a need to invest in the stock market but do not feel comfortable picking stocks or trading options, then there is no better way to invest than via mutual funds.

In order to buy and sell index funds or mutual funds it does require that you have an account with a broker such as TD Ameritrade, TD Trade King, E*Trade, Scottrade and so on. Mutual fund investing is best for beginners who don't want to worry about economic events that affect stocks and might lose money if they became emotional during times like these. Buying into mutual funds is great for many investors to start off with because if they don't have time to do the research and buy stocks then investing in mutual funds can diversify their portfolio of stocks and help them feel more comfortable.

When buying an index fund or a mutual fund there are three different types to choose from. The first type is called an "*open-ended*" fund which means that anyone can buy and sell at any time during the day however those who buy or sell on the open market will not receive as favorable of a price as those who invest directly from the company's website.

- The second type is called a *"closed-ended"* fund which means that they only offer a limited number of shares. Once these shares have sold, which can take days or even weeks, the fund will no longer allow anyone to buy into it.

- The third and best way to buy an index fund or mutual fund is called a *"no-load"* fund. A no-load fund is exactly what it says, you will NEVER pay any fees in order to invest in this specific mutual fund. Those who invest in a no-load index fund or mutual fund will receive the same price that the company receives for selling shares.

One very important thing to realize is that it takes money to make money. It doesn't make any sense to buy an index fund and hold onto it for ten years if you are not going to reinvest any of the gains from your initial investment into more shares of the same mutual fund. Therefore, it is a good idea to invest enough money in an index fund or mutual fund so that you can purchase additional shares every time you have excess capital since no one can predict what the stock market will do over a long period of time.

There are different types of index funds and mutual funds to invest in:

- The first type is called an *"Index Fund"* which tracks an index such as the S&P 500, Dow Jones 30 Industrial Average or the NASDAQ Composite. These funds will hold every single stock that is in the index which means that it diversifies your holdings by spreading your money across thousands of stocks. This is one of the most important factors of a mutual fund because just because one stock performed poorly over a period of time does not mean that every other stock in the index fund will do poorly as well. Therefore, since you are diversifying your holdings by buying thousands of different stocks with just a couple hundred dollars you will experience less volatility in your portfolio.

- The second type of mutual fund is called a *"Dividend Income Fund".* These funds will invest in dividend-paying stocks such as those which pay dividends in order to provide their investors with income. Usually these funds will have a large portion of their holdings in utility companies, real estate companies and even some healthcare stocks.

- The third type of mutual fund is called an *"Active Management Fund"* which means that the manager of the fund can make different types of investments other than buying all of the stocks in the index. The active management fund can also buy bonds, foreign currencies or even commodities within your portfolio.

The last type of mutual fund is called a "Fund of Funds" which means that it contains different types of mutual funds. When investing in a fund of funds you should look for one that has several different types of funds so that your money is protected against poor performance in one specific fund or index.

Once you have decided to invest in an index fund or mutual fund then the easiest way to purchase shares would be through the company directly since they will charge you less fees. However, if you don't have enough money to make a direct investment then there is another way to invest. You can always start with a small amount of money and then reinvest the gains from your initial investment in the same mutual fund.

If you are just starting out in the stock market it is important that you do not buy an index fund or mutual fund without knowing what it does. Every mutual fund will usually have a prospectus which explains everything about that specific index fund or mutual fund. If there are any questions about the fund, then you should follow up with a phone call to the company.

CHAPTER 9. EXCHANGE-TRADED FUNDS (ETFS)

There has been a lot of buzz around ETFs in the media lately. You may have read, for instance, that they can offer diversification and lower costs. And that's true—but it's not the whole story! ETFs are investment funds that track an index, commodity or other benchmark. They trade like stocks on an exchange and seek to match their performance without any added management fees-making them a great option for individual investors who want to minimize trading costs. But similar to most investment vehicles, ETFs have some unique pros and cons. Here's what investors should know to make educated decisions about whether these funds are right for them.

What Makes an ETF Different?

ETFs are not mutual funds or other types of managed products such as exchange-traded notes (ETNs). They are structured to track a particular investment benchmark instead of seeking to outperform it. For example, an ETF may hold stocks or bonds that are included in the S&P 500 index. Another way to think about it is that benchmarks usually represent a diversified basket of securities within a particular category and are generally calculated and maintained by third parties such as an index provider (e.g. MSCI, the Federal Reserve, etc.) For example: an ETF might hold a handful of stocks it believes to be representative of the S&P 500 index, or even all 500 stocks. It only seeks to match what the index has done during the prior trading day by providing investors with an intraday return equal to that of the benchmark on a given day.

So, What's in an ETF?

ETFs are generally structured as Unit Investment Trusts (UITs), which means they're open-ended and ongoing vehicles that issue redeemable shares. They can invest in anything from equities and bonds to metals and commodities. They are also passively managed and their portfolios are valued daily because they're traded on an exchange. Some ETFs even provide the ability to short specific securities or indexes, giving investors more flexibility. Exchange-Traded Funds are a type of mutual fund that can be traded like stocks. It is an investment that provides diversified exposure to assets such as stocks, bonds, or commodities. There are many ETFs and they come in different shapes and sizes with various strategies, which means it may take some time to figure out what you're looking for.

Here we are going to discuss different types of Exchange-Traded Funds to give you a general idea of what they are and why you might use them.

Index ETFs

Index ETFs passively track an underlying index. For example, the Standard and Poor's 500 Index, which is comprised of the largest companies in the US market by market capitalization listed on the NYSE or NASDAQ.

When you invest in an index ETF, you are investing in a basket of securities representing that particular index. Therefore, if your investment goes up then it's because your underlying basket did well too whether it's based on investable indexes such as bond indexes or non-investable indexes such as commodity indexes.

ETFs That Aim to Track a Specific Index and Outperform It

These ETFs hold the underlying securities in the same proportion as they appear in the index, but they are designed to outperform it. This means that if, for example, you're expecting a large capital gain in a particular sector then you'd want to buy an ETF that aims to track the benchmark but with less volatility. For example, you might invest in an ETF that tracks the S&P 500 Index but invests 75% of its holdings in stocks with above-average fundamentals such as high earnings growth and low debt.

Sector Funds — US-Based Indexes

These aim to track a specific sector such as technology or health care. If you are looking to invest in a specific sector, then you might want to consider an ETF that bets on one of these sectors.

Broadly Diversified ETFs

These are similar to index ETFs and hold a basket of assets and track the index but have a broader spectrum of holdings. While this means more diversification, it also means less individual stock research is required. An investor who does not want to spend much time monitoring his investments may prefer this type of fund.

Managed ETFs

These are actively managed ETFs. They require the work of an investment manager to oversee their holdings and are not tied to a particular index.

In summary, if you're looking for a simple way to invest in stocks and bonds then consider using an ETF; however, be sure to do your research before making any final decisions about which type of ETF is right for you and, perhaps more importantly, how to buy them. As the number of Exchange-Traded Funds increases so does the number of ways for investors to trade them, including direct access trading as well as traditional brokers and advisors. It is also possible to trade an ETF in a tax-advantaged account such as a 401(k) or an IRA (using a Traditional or Roth IRA). This may allow for some tax advantages that would be unavailable from using other investment vehicles.

Apart from the bid-ask spread, investors should consider brokerage and transfer fees, which can vary depending on the selected trading platform. In addition, additional fees may apply when investing in specific ETFs. For example, some types of ETFs have higher per-trade commissions than others.

In addition, if an investor plans to trade frequently or reinvest his dividends (a common strategy) he could incur significant transaction costs in a short period if he chooses to use a brokerage firm that offers low trading commissions for individual trades.

ETFs can be held alongside other investments such as mutual funds or stocks. This makes them useful in constructing a well-rounded portfolio that offers diversification and liquidity to investors. However, not all ETFs can be freely bought and sold in an investor's brokerage account. Those that are listed on exchanges must meet certain requirements and therefore have more liquidity than others, which may only be available to trade via order book at major brokerage houses (for example, Guggenheim S&P 500 Equal Weight ETF (RSP)). Other widely traded U.S. ETFs include the iShares Core S&P Mid-Cap ETF (IJH), which tracks the S&P MidCap 400 index, and the iShares Russell 2000 ETF (IWM), which tracks the Russell 2000 Index. ETFs may appeal to certain investors who want to invest in a specific sector or country, but lack sufficient capital or time to build a portfolio of individual securities. By using an ETF, an investor can quickly assemble a diverse basket of securities that track specific markets such as oil and gas drilling companies or an entire nation's stock market. Now let us explore when one should buy and sell Exchange-Traded Funds (ETFs).

ETFs have been around for almost two decades and they are quickly becoming mainstream. In fact, ETFs now represent one of the most important financial investment products in the marketplace.

Some investors use ETFs as a way to gain exposure to different securities such as commodities, stocks or bonds—all with just one trade. An investor may want exposure to a particular industry sector but does not want the risk that comes with individual stock ownership. The investor can purchase an index-based ETF that tracks a specific group of securities providing diversification benefits in this manner.

While there are many different ETFs out there, they can be grouped into three main categories: Equity ETFs; Fixed Income ETFs; Commodity ETFs.

Within each of these categories are numerous sub-categories. Here is a sampling:

Equity ETFs

- Global Equity (including emerging markets)
- Large Cap Value (e.g., iShares S&P 500 Value Index Fund)
- Mid Cap (e.g., iShares S&P MidCap Index Fund)
- Small Cap (e.g., iShares Russell 2000 Index Fund)
- Industrials (e.g. Power Shares Dynamic Industrials Portfolio)
- Real Estate (e.g., Market Vectors Retail REIT ETF)

Fixed Income ETFs

- US treasury (e.g., iShares iBoxx T-Bond Index Fund) — This is a good way to play the changing interest rate environment.
- High Yield (e.g., Direxion Daily 20+ Year Treasury Bear 3X Shares) — This is a good way to play the credit markets including financial stocks.

- Municipal Bonds (e.g. iShares S&P National AMT-Free Muni Bond Index Fund) — This is a good way to play the municipal bond market.

Commodity ETFs

- Energy (e.g., Market Vectors Oil Refiners ETF) — This is a good way to play the energy sector.

- Precious Metals (e.g., SPDR Gold Shares) — This is a good way to play the precious metal sector.

- Agriculture (e.g., Power Shares DB Agriculture Fund) — This is a good way to play the agriculture sector.

As one can see, ETFs can be used in numerous ways for a variety of purposes. The question is: When should one buy or sell an ETF?

The general consensus is that if an individual investor would like to invest in the stock market but does not want to actually buy and sell stocks outright, then an ETF product may be the right investment vehicle. Likewise, if someone wants exposure to commodities—but does not want to actually buy and sell physical gold, silver or soybeans—then a commodity ETF will provide this type of exposure. If you are buying a particular ETF for the long-term and mean to keep it there until you need your money, then you can hold on until retirement. On the other hand, if you plan to trade more actively and have the time to do so, then there may be times when you should buy and sell ETFs.

For example, if stock markets enter a prolonged down cycle, an investor may decide to get out there and buy stocks at these lower levels after a correction in order to replace those stocks that are now underperforming their benchmarks. At such a time, selling their ETF shares and buying individual stocks would provide this type of exposure. There was one particular individual who bought shares in a small-cap value ETF against the advice of many Wall Street professionals. He held his position during the 2008 market crash and today is one of the most over-leveraged, but also one of the most profitable investors out there.

Conversely, if markets are going up for an extended period of time as they have been in recent years, an ETF investor may decide to get out there and sell their holdings in order to take profits. Again, selling their shares and buying individual stocks would provide such exposure. In recent years, we have seen many investors who sold their holdings of small-cap value ETFs in order to buy large-cap value stocks (e.g., iShares Russell 2000 Value Index Fund vs iShares S&P 500 Value Index Fund). While this strategy is a great way to hedge one's bet, it is not advisable to make such drastic changes all at once.

While there are several risks and complexities associated with investing in ETFs, individuals who take the time to educate themselves on what they are buying should be able to avoid some of the pitfalls. What is important is that investors in ETFs remember that these investments are not immune to extreme downward changes just because they may have done well over the long term.

CHAPTER 10. OTHER TYPES OF INVESTMENTS

Cryptocurrencies

Cryptocurrencies are a medium of exchange using cryptography to secure transactions, control the creation of additional units, and authenticate the transfer of assets. Cryptocurrencies let buyers and sellers conduct financial transactions without revealing their identities. By decentralizing public transaction data, cryptocurrencies eliminate the need for third-party checking and verification.

The first cryptocurrency to capture popular attention was Bitcoin, which was launched in 2009 by an individual or group operating under the name Satoshi Nakamoto. Like other currencies, Bitcoins are not backed by a physical commodity but rather by a peer-to-peer network of computers users who use the coins as money.

What Is Bitcoin?

Bitcoin was introduced on 31 October 2008 to a cryptography mailing list, and released as open-source software in 2009. It is a cryptocurrency, so-called because it uses cryptography to control the creation of its units of currency and verify the transfer of assets. Bitcoin transactions are irreversible and immune to fraudulent chargebacks. The system is peer-to-peer and transactions take place between users directly through the use of cryptography.

If you are looking for the top places to buy and sell Cryptocurrencies, this article provides a list of the best cryptocurrency exchanges. The Bitcoin market is an important space that has been sending traders scrambling in search of a reliable exchange platform. If you want to invest in cryptocurrencies, then there are five exchanges on which you can do so: Coinbase, Bit stamp, Kraken, Bitfinex and Poloniex.

You may not be familiar with all of these platforms as they tend to cater to more tech-savvy traders. What's interesting about each is that they vary in their approach to how you buy and sell cryptocurrencies—in other words what currencies they offer and how advanced their trading infrastructure is.

Gold and Silver

Investing in physical gold and silver is a tangible, proven strategy to hedge against economic uncertainty. It cannot be stolen like the cash in your bank account, and it doesn't need an internet connection to retain its value. Gold and silver are liquid assets that can be conveniently transformed into cash at any time, with no restrictive holding periods or costs.

Many people put off purchasing physical gold or silver because they feel it's a complicated process that requires significant research or expertise, but the truth is that you don't need any special skills or training to get started investing in physical gold and silver.

Gold is primarily an investment whereas silver is primarily industrial. Quite simply, gold has a far greater store of value as a raw commodity than silver does. However, because it is primarily an investment rather than an industrial metal, it can experience swings in price more dramatically than the price fluctuations experienced by silver, which is used more for practical purposes such as jewelry or in medicine.

Precious metals purchased through your brokerage account with a bank or credit union may be covered by the Federal Deposit Insurance Corp., but check with the company first. Insurance payouts can take up to 60 days; the metal itself is typically received in three days.

Private Equity

Private equity has been around since the 1970s, but for some reason these days it is getting a lot of attention. Private equity is a type of investment fund that uses investors' money to buy companies. It can seem intimidating to figure out when and where to buy and sell private equity — but if you are looking to make some money, this post will bring you up-to-speed on the basics and help you get started. Private equity is a straightforward concept. A private equity fund is almost exactly the same as any other investment fund (like a mutual fund or hedge fund)—it just invests in a slightly different type of investment.

As with other types of funds, private equity funds will be bought and sold on stock exchanges. You can use exchange-traded funds (ETFs) to invest in large private equity firms like Blackstone and TPG Capital. For traders, the ETFs for Blackstone and TPG Capital are BXLT and TPLM, respectively.

If you are looking to buy individual stocks, you can look into stocks of smaller companies that are held by private equity firms. For example, Marriott, Hyatt and Hilton are all owned by private equity firms like Blackstone.

The biggest drawback to private equity investing is that it is a lot riskier.

If you are invested in a mutual fund that owns stock, the worst-case scenario is a complete loss of your investment—but this would be extremely rare because most companies do not go completely bankrupt. In contrast, private equity funds can lose all of their money and often times will.

And even though private equity funds are a type of investment fund and have the same risk/reward characteristic as other types of investment funds, they are taxed differently.

Rather than being taxed only when you sell your investment (like mutual funds), private equity is taxed on a yearly basis—the amount invested plus profit is considered income each year.

Hedge Funds

Hedge funds is an industry that deals in the regulation of investments and speculation. The hedge fund industry has experienced significant growth in recent years, with over 8,000 hedge funds managing about $3 trillion in assets as of December 2013. This article aims to provide a brief overview of the historical background, descriptions, advantages and disadvantages of hedge funds as well as the potential risks involved with this type of investment vehicles. Hedge Funds, or funds of hedge funds, are investment vehicles that are made out of investments in other investment companies. The most common form of a hedge fund is a pooled investment vehicle with the goal to reduce risk by using an array of investments and trading strategies. Hedge funds have been used since 1954 and were created because conventional publicly traded securities were producing less than satisfactory returns. The goal is to make as much money as possible while also ensuring that the investor does not lose any money on bad trades. A hedge fund manager is a person who earns money via performance fees, incentive compensation, and trading profits.

Ethical Investments

Ethical investing is a technique where an investor picks investment dependent on an individual ethical code. Ethical investing endeavors to help enterprises having a constructive outcome, for example, manageable energy, and make an investment return. With an increment in ESG assets, there are more ethical investments than any other time in recent memory. Obviously, what is "ethical" relies upon the individual. What is ethical to you may not be to another person. That is the reason it is essential to look in the background of ethical investments and ensure they line up with the effect you would prefer to have. While no investment is ensured, the exhibition of ethical assets has been demonstrated to be like the presentation of customary assets—truth be told, some exploration shows that ethical asset execution might be predominant. As indicated by Morningstar information, maintainable assets beat their conventional friends in 2019, with 66% completing the year with returns in the top portion of their Morningstar classes. There is likewise some proof that recommends that ethical assets may offer lower levels of market hazard than customary assets, even in unstable markets, for example, the plunge during the initial many months of the COVID-19 pandemic. As indicated by Morningstar information, 24 out of 26 ESG list supports outflanked tantamount ordinary assets during the main quarter of 2020.

Coins, Stamps and Art

Coins

Coins are well-known investments, but they can often be hard to come by. One of the most popular ones for collectors are US pennies before the year 1982. Most will start at about $5 and increase at about 10% per year—depending on the date you buy one and when you sell it. Most people don't keep track of coins for their entire life, so when they're found in old furniture or wallets, the owner will sell them to a coin collector.

Stamps

Stamps are another collectible. They aren't as popular as coins or other collectibles because they're fairly easy to find, but for stamps issued after 1989 (when they stopped using the mail system to sell them), you can expect an increase in value of about 10% per year.

Art

If you are in the mood to invest in something more artistic, then art might be just the thing. The timelessness of great works of art is legendary, so the investment potential is gigantic. There are other reasons to invest in art, too.

For example, if your home or office has a limited amount of wall space, buying an art piece will add value to the environment—and if you are not able to repay your loan on the art, then you can just sell it again later and recoup some of your losses. Are you looking for ways to invest your money? Coins, stamps and art are three ways to consider. Collectible coins can be a solid investment when done strategically. Stamps can also provide an interesting opportunity if you know how to buy and sell them effectively. Finally, art has always been viewed as one of the most lucrative investments out there, though many people don't see it as a realistic option for their budgets.

The Purchase of Comic Books

Comic books are exciting and fun. They bring out the imagination, and some of them even have their own movie. Interestingly enough, most people who read them know little about the process of producing comic books these days. Though they remain popular, the industry itself is not as lucrative as it was in years past. The irony is that people will continue to buy comics whether they are produced by Marvel or DC Comics or some other company. They are an industry investment that can result in nice profits depending on how long you hold onto them. There is a tremendous amount of risk involved with buying comic books for investment purposes because they can be lost easily. You may have had this happen to you or someone you know in the past. They go into storage for years and get damaged or destroyed completely. You don't want this to happen with your comic books because of the money that is tied up in them and their future potential value.

One of the best ways to invest in comic books without having to worry about storage is through one of the current comic book dealers on the market who takes care of storing your comic books for a monthly fee, rather than having you store them yourself. You will not have to worry about collecting them anymore, and it also ensures that they will not be lost forever.

CHAPTER 11. HOW TO MANAGE YOUR INVESTMENT PORTFOLIO

Managing an investment portfolio is an important skill for any young investor to learn. The main reason is that, as you get older, you will be able to acquire more capital to invest. Investing during your teen years will provide you with the opportunity to learn important skills that you can use when managing your own investment portfolio later in life.

To get started, let's start by examining the basics of what an investment portfolio is, and what it takes to manage one successfully. Then we can look at how these skills can be acquired by a young investor like yourself.

What Is an Investment Portfolio?

An investment portfolio is basically everything that you own that has value (either tangible or intangible). For example, if you owned a car it would be part of your investment portfolio. If you owned a $100 bill, that would also be part of your investment portfolio. Even if you have no money invested yet, the time that you spend working on your education (and the knowledge that results) is also an investment and therefore part of an investment portfolio.

The recent bear market has shaken many investors' confidence. Having lived through the previous bear market from 1973 to 1974, there are some investors who are perhaps feeling a bit anxious about how they will handle a similar scenario in the future. In this section, we will look at how management of your portfolio can help you manage your nerves during periods of market volatility.

There are two basic ways to manage an investment portfolio: (1) You can stay invested no matter what happens in the market, or (2) you can time your moves based on market conditions and try to capture gains when you think a rally is coming. Let's take a look at these two strategies and see which may work best for you.

Strategy #1:

Stay Invested All the Time

This strategy suggests that investors stay invested all the time, and worry only about managing their portfolio with new contributions and rebalancing their holdings periodically. This is probably the more passive approach, and doesn't require you to read The Wall Street Journal every day. It also helps remove some of the emotion from investing decisions. The idea is that over the long term, if you hold a diversified portfolio of stocks, bonds, and cash equivalents (T-Bills), your investments will behave in a predictable manner, allowing you to ignore daily market fluctuations. You just check how your investments are doing every once in a while. The major drawback to this approach is that you will have to weather some very difficult periods. For example, consider the year 2000 when the NASDAQ plunged nearly 50% in just over a year. A portfolio in just the S&P 500 Index would have dropped about 30% during that same period. If you were holding all your investments in stocks at that time, it would have been very difficult to stick with your plan and stay invested all the way through until 2002.

Strategy #2:

Try to Time the Market

The second strategy is to try and time the market. This approach involves having a well-developed understanding of current economic conditions, an understanding of how these conditions are impacting the markets, and then making your buying and selling decisions based on that knowledge. The basic idea is that if you can figure out the best times to buy and sell, you will be able to outperform the market over time.

In order to implement this strategy successfully, you need considerable expertise in financial analysis. You also need a lot of patience because short-term results will vary significantly with each decision on when to buy or sell. For example, let's assume that you had correctly guessed that the stock market was going to start recovering in April 2003. You could then have liquidated your stocks and invested in a short-term government bond fund. In April 2003, the Vanguard Short-Term Government Bond Index Fund (NYSE: VFSUX) yielded 3.01%, which was significantly better than the 2.37% you would have earned from an S&P 500 index fund during that same period. The problem with this type of move is that if you were wrong about rising stocks, then you would have paid a big price for your mistake. For example, if you had sold your stocks and invested in the bond fund in April 2002, you would have lost about 7% over the next 10 months.

As you can see, there is a very fine line between successfully timing the market and simply guessing wrong. To succeed at this game over time requires a huge amount of knowledge about economic conditions and market trends, as well as a tolerance for short-term losses when you are wrong. Even then, trying to time the market isn't for everybody. It is a very challenging approach that requires a lot of effort.

So which approach is best? The answer depends on your personality type. If you have the ability to read the market and understand how current economic conditions will impact your investments, then timing the market will give you a better chance of long-term success. If that is too difficult for you, then sticking with your long-term plan and just checking in from time to time might be a better way to go.

CHAPTER 12. PERSONAL ADVISOR AND ONLINE BROKERS

Your financial security is important. However, for some of us, it can be an area we find difficult to understand and manage. That's why so many of us turn to an advisor—someone who has experience in these areas and can help you make decisions that will keep your finances on the right track. So what are your options?

A personal advisor is a good option for people who would like one-on-one guidance with their finances. They will typically take a comprehensive approach, looking at all aspects of your financial life from debt to taxes to savings. Personal advisors might charge by the hour or they might have a set monthly fee, depending on their arrangement with you. *Benefits:* A personal advisor will look at your whole financial picture and help you make decisions that are right for your life situation. You will have one primary point person who is available to you and to whom you can build a relationship. *Potential drawbacks:* Personal advisors are often expensive, though they might be willing to offer a free consultation in order to win your business.

An online broker is an automated way to invest that comes with the expertise and industry contacts of an independent investment firm. The internet-based platforms for these types of accounts are easy to use, but they also offer personalized advice from expert analysts who can help you choose the investments that best fit your goals. *Benefits:* Online brokers can be a good option for people who are comfortable doing their own financial research but want help from people with experience. These types of advisors can allow you to invest on your own, but also give you the benefit of a team behind the scenes that can offer advice and answer questions. *Potential drawbacks:* If you are nervous about investing without seeing what you are buying, this is not for you. There is no ability to ask the analyst for advice; an online platform makes recommendations based on your goals and risk tolerance. Every day, consumers are bombarded with messages from online brokers and advisors. With so many different solutions to choose from, it is hard for people to know which one is best. Additionally, the products they offer are typically not easy to compare because there are no universal standards in the financial industry. This makes selecting an advisor and broker very challenging for people who are new to investing or don't have time to research all the options themselves. Putting together this brief article has thus become a necessity because we understand first-hand how overwhelming this process can be. We've gone through it too, and have put together some helpful tips that make the comparison easier. If you're planning to use any of the services listed in this report, you should pay attention to the following factors:

1) **Education.** The first and most important thing to check is educational background. Does it have any? What are they? These degrees will tell you what kind of investor the advisor is. For example, if it has a finance-related degree, such as MSc in Financial Analysis or Certified Financial Planner, then it can give you an idea of whether it will be able to provide intelligent and relevant advice. For people who want a more personal touch in their lives, such as with health or relationship issues, a Master's degree in psychology or social work may be best for them.

2) **Experience.** The second most important factor is how long has the advisor been in business. You want someone who has been established and remained relevant for at least a few years, because this shows it has survived and grown based on the quality of service it provides.

3) **Licenses and Insurance.** Brokers can be certified by organizations such as Chartered Financial Analyst (CFA), Certified Financial Planner (CFP), Chartered Life Underwriter (CLU), Chartered Life Specialist (CLS) or Registered Investment Advisor (RIA). They ensure that a professional follow certain ethical standard and maintain a proper level of education required to serve you better.

Most of the time, these credentials mean the advisor is an experienced professional in the industry. But it doesn't mean they are a good fit for you. They are just a sign that you can trust what they offer because these licenses have qualifications that can only be gained through meaningful coursework and relevant experience. It is also important to double-check that your advisors carry liability insurance and fidelity bond, which protect you if something goes wrong. The reason you need to be cautious about this is because there are some dishonest individuals in the financial world who may wish to take advantage of unwary customers. The best way to avoid this is to only deal with well-established and reputable brokers.

4) **Tax Filing Services.** Many people do not consider the importance of picking a qualified tax filing service, which is only natural because most of us do not like dealing with numbers, especially when it comes to taxes. But tax filing services are important because they can help make sure you stay on top of your taxes and also ensure that you're not audited by the government for paying too

little or too much in taxes. This will save a lot of headaches for you over the years, as running afoul with the IRS can result in a painful consequence if you fail to pay them properly or handle your expenses incorrectly.

5) **Investment Portfolio**. Some brokers are solely online investment platforms and do not offer any other services. On the other hand, some of them manage funds and stocks directly for you as a customer. This requires special licensing and also brings with its certain risks, so you want to make sure you choose a solution that is most appropriate for your unique needs.

6) **Commissions and Fees.** While the commissions may vary from one broker to another, the main thing you need to look at is whether or not they charge fees on top of their commissions. This can be quite costly over time because it can add up exponentially if you do not check or evaluate your portfolio often enough. This is why it's better to go with a broker that only charges commissions, which will not cost you anything else.

7) **Brokerage Accounts and Products.** As for the products they offer, many brokers have low or no-minimum requirements, which is great because it ensures more people can get into the market without having to make a large upfront investment.

8) **Customer Service.** Lastly, do they have good customer service? All companies offer some form of customer support these days, but some of these are just unaccountably bad—so much so that it seems like they do not care about their clients at all. This is why you should really make sure the company you're dealing with has good customer service, which should be both prompt and thorough.

A good broker will not just find you the right financial products to invest in, but will also help you monitor your investment portfolio as well as provide education every step of the way. This will ensure that your investments grow steadily and without any undue risk. The end goal is to have a steady stream of passive income for retirement that allows you to comfortably live out the last years of your life in peace and happiness.

How to Open a Broker Account

Opening a broker account is very simple; all you need to provide is basic information (name and address) and then deposit money into the account so that you are able to start trading with real money on the market. You'll need to provide your social security number (or your tax id) and agree to the terms of service. After filling that out, you'll be brought to a page that asks for your financial account information. Make sure you only put in information for whatever bank or brokerage account you want to deposit money into! After completing these steps, check your email to confirm your Account information. Finally, you'll get into page where you will be able to deposit money into your brokerage account. I recommend depositing $500 or more but at least $100 so that you are able to start trading on the market. This is an easy way for us introduce you to investing with a Broker Account. You can read through the rest of websites to learn more about it if you want.

CHAPTER 13. BEST INVESTING AND MICRO-SAVINGS APPS

The world is changing. People are working more and more hours on two jobs. There is less time to do things that you enjoy and too much work to do in your spare time.

Many people have no choice but to work hard for the money, but there is still a choice about how you invest that money, which can make all the difference in your future financial health.

Investing Vs Micro-Savings Apps

We have been taught that the stock market is how you make money. However, it has become increasingly difficult to access stock market investments and sometimes even to understand them.

The methods that used to work aren't as reliable as they used to be, and investing in individual stocks can be risky.

The other alternative is micro-savings apps—which in our opinion are less work, more convenient and more secure than stock trading/investing. They also have the potential for being much more profitable in the long-term because of their compound interest rate multipliers built in. This means your money really grows on itself and the more it makes, the more it can make. This is as opposed to stock market investments in which you must wait for a company to pay out dividends (if they do) or sell your stock at a profit.

In addition, micro-savings apps can be used and accessed from anywhere in the world with an internet connection, so you can invest your money from anywhere without having to deal with geographical restrictions.

The Best Micro-Savings Apps

We have chosen these apps by considering budget, time available to make money, acquired financial experience and of course their potential return on investment.

1. Acorns

With Acorns, you can invest your money as frequently as you want and have it automatically withdrawn from your debit card or bank account.

The Acorns "Roundup" feature allows customers to make micro-savings for free each time they shop at a retailer with a supported credit or debit card, without changing their shopping habits. Whenever a purchase is made, the app rounds up to the nearest dollar and invests the remaining change into an Acorns portfolio. Acorns have also partnered with influential business leaders such as Yahoo CEO Marissa Mayer and Uber board member Bill Gurley to offer challenges that can earn its users additional cash rewards for investing early, often, and responsibly.

Additionally, the app has an easy-to-understand and user-friendly interface that makes it accessible to new investors.

The only drawback is fees—Acorns charges $1 a month for balances under $5,000 (or 0.25% of assets per year); $2 a month for balances above that threshold (or 0.25%). You can also try out Acorns' free version for 14 days.

2. Stash

Stash's goal is to make investing simple and cost-effective. The app serves as a platform for every type of investment from trading stocks, to spending your spare change. Unlike other apps on the market, Stash offers customers the ability to choose how they want to invest their money—by selecting an area of personal interest like "politics" or "sports".

If you are not sure where to start, the app will also suggest a portfolio based on your age and financial goals.

Initially launched in 2015, Stash has gone through several iterations in terms of features and functionality with its newest release in March 2017.

The current version of the app allows users to:

- Invest as little as $5 at a time across hundreds of different investments (no minimum balance requirement).

- Decide how they wish to be billed (quarterly, monthly and yearly).

- Link up a bank account or debit card for easy and convenient automated investing.

- Choose from hundreds of stocks, bonds, ETFs, and cryptocurrencies.

Recent updates to the app include "Watch-lists"—which allow users to track relevant stocks and cryptocurrencies in real-time. Stash also offers educational tools like "Stash Academy"—a personal finance library with articles related to money management. For those who want more information about the principles behind investing their money, "Stash University" is an interactive investing course that walks users through key concepts like diversification and risk tolerance.

3. Acorns Spend

Acorns recently launched Acorns Spend, a free app that is similar to the original app, but instead of investing your money, you can save it with it. Though the two apps have similarities—like round-up and invest features and checklists—they differ in the fact that Acorns Spend allows customers to spend their spare change without having to make adjustments to their financial habits. With a linked debit or credit card, Acorns Spend round up your purchases like Acorns and invests the change using the same investment portfolio found in its other app, while also eating into your debit or credit card's budget. What sets this app apart from the competition is its generous savings potential—users can save up to 5.4% or $1,215 a year for someone making $50,000 annually—based on the app's tax efficiency algorithm. The algorithm works by identifying financial opportunities and effectively minimizing your tax obligations by maximizing your pre-tax dollars. Another feature that sets Acorns Spend apart from other apps of its kind is the fact that it allows customers to spend their money in real-time without any account minimums or monthly fees for balances under $5,000 (or 0.25% of assets per year). However, if users are looking to invest their savings instead of spending them, they will have to upgrade to the regular Acorns or Acorns Later app.

4. Tiller

Tiller provides a service called "Bill Paying Made Simple". According to the company's website:

"Tiller is a smart, easy to use personal finance manager that gives you the tools to better understand and manage your money. With Tiller, you can quickly see where your money is going and take control without spending tons of time analyzing spreadsheets or inputting data."

Here's how it works: Customers pay certain bills from their checking accounts (i.e. rent, credit cards bills, car loans, etc.) through their Tiller account for free with no fees. There are different tiers of service offered by Tiller depending on what you pay them each month.

For example, the most basic level of service costs $2.50 per month for customers who pay an average of $500 per month in bills through the service.

The second-tier costs $4.95 a month for customers with monthly payments totaling more than $1,000. The third level charges 5.95 monthly for those who pay more than $5,000 in bills a month through the service.

Using Tiller to pay bills can save you money.

It might not seem like paying a few bucks to save yourself hours of work is worth it but when you consider all the time you'll save over your lifetime on tedious tasks, it is well worth it. The company is also taking longer to achieve profit-making status. In 1998 and 1999, 89% of the companies funded by venture capitalists went public or were acquired within 4 years. This year, the figure was 64%.

The shift from initial public offerings to mergers may reflect an increase in Internet companies that are not yet profitable but have strong brand names and sites with loyal users. For example, Amazon.com Inc. was able to raise $54 million in its 1997 initial public offering, but it had annual losses of about $500,000 before it began posting profits. The company grew quickly and in March 2000, less than a year after going public, Amazon agreed to be acquired by online bookseller Barnes & Noble for $1.45 billion.

"We're in the second wave of venture-capital investing," *says Michael Sinkin, who runs Red Mile Group Inc., an e-commerce consulting firm in New York.* "It's much more likely now that venture capitalists will make money through an acquisition. It's harder to make money through an IPO."

The second wave may last longer, too. *"In the 1990s,"* says Mr. Sinkin, *"I'd see venture capitalists get excited about a new idea and try it out. If it didn't work, they'd fold up and move on to something else."* Now that e-commerce and e-business are mature industries, people expect to spend years working on them. There is little doubt that the venture capitalists will be along for the ride. In the meantime, they are making money from companies like Tiller. The company charges a monthly fee of $2.50 to $5.95 for its services, but the savings can far outweigh the costs. For example, instead of letting your landlord collect your rent on a monthly basis by sending you a check or charging it to your credit card, you can have all of your rent automatically withdrawn from your checking account and sent directly to him or her—and save yourself the transaction fee and the time spent writing out checks. Here is how it works: You can use Tiller to pay all federal bills that charge a flat fee plus postage (such as income tax payments). You can also ask any company that sends invoices to you (such as your cable-TV provider) whether it will accept payments through Tiller. Once you have set up a biller on Tiller, you can pay your bills right through your bank account.

5. Robinhood Financial (Formerly "Robinhood")

The Robinhood app, which lets users to trade U.S. stocks for free, provides an easy-to-use platform that can help anyone learn the basics of investing in the stock market and save money on commissions.

The app is fairly intuitive—users can tap on a company's name to see how it's performing or tap on the menu icon to view all available stocks and options and their respective prices in real-time (unlike other apps that only provide stock information).

6. M1 Finance

Founded in 2014 by Alex Friedman and Jacob Gibson, M1 Finance is a free mobile app that allows customers to manage and invest their money. Similar to Robinhood, M1 offers commission-free trading on thousands of ETFs and stocks with no minimum account balance required.

The app's tax optimization feature helps customers maximize the after-tax growth potential of their investments by identifying cost basis.

Even though it is free to use, M1 charges a fee of $0.0035 for every stock trade and an ETF trading fee of $0.0025 for every share traded.

M1 also offers a "Smart Deposit" feature that automatically invests the money users deposit into their M1 account into their respective investment portfolios. The more money customers deposit into their accounts, the more money they will have in their investment portfolios (up to $15,000).

The company offers taxable users two custodial accounts: one with short-term capital gains and one with long-term capital gains.

One drawback for M1 is that users have to manually invest their money, which is an annoyance for those who don't have a solid understanding of investments and trading. Another drawback is that there isn't a mobile-based app to manage accounts from iOS devices. However, M1 does have an iPhone app, but it doesn't look as polished as Robinhood's.

CHAPTER 14. MISTAKES TO AVOID

Five Huge Mistakes that Beginners Make

I get many messages each day from merchants and investors, a large number of whom have quite recently committed one of the errors that I talk about in this section. In the event that you can keep away from these slip-ups when you are simply beginning, you will be path in front of the pack and will likewise save yourself a ton of misfortunes and wretchedness.

1. Try not to purchase stocks that are hitting 52-week lows

We have just examined this point, however it bears rehashing, in light of the fact that such countless new brokers lose a ton of cash attempting to get the famous "falling blade". Notwithstanding what everybody will advise you, you are quite often much better purchasing a stock that is hitting 52-week highs than one hitting 52-week lows.

Has an organization that you own just announced some truly downright terrible? Assuming this is the case, recollect that there will never be only one cockroach. Awful news comes in bunches.

Numerous investors as of late scholarly this the most difficult way possible with General Electric, which just continued announcing something terrible after another, making the stock slump from 30 to 7. There is nothing of the sort as a "protected stock". Even a blue-chip stock can go down a great deal on the off chance that it loses its upper hand or the organization settles on awful choices.

A course of terrible news can regularly make a stock pattern down or hold down more than once. In the event that you own a stock that does this, it is frequently better to get out and stand by a couple of months (or years) to reappear. Again, there will never be only one cockroach.

2. Try not to exchange penny stocks

A penny stock is any stock that exchanges under $5. Except if you are a high-level broker, you ought to stay away from all penny stocks. I would stretch out this by urging you to likewise evade all stocks estimated under $10. Regardless of whether you have a little exchanging account ($5,000) or less, you are in an ideal situation purchasing less portions of a more expensive stock than a great deal of portions of a penny stock.

That is on the grounds that low-estimated stocks are frequently connected with lower quality organizations. Thus, they are not for the most part permitted to exchange on the NYSE or the NASDAQ. All things considered, they exchange on the OTCBB ("over the counter notice board") or Pink Sheets, the two of which have considerably less rigid monetary announcing prerequisites than the significant trades do.

A considerable lot of these organizations have never made a benefit. They might be fakes or shell organizations that are planned exclusively to improve the board and different insiders. They may likewise incorporate previous "blue-chips" that have run into some bad luck like Eastman Kodak or Lehman Brothers.

What's more, penny stocks are characteristically more unstable than more extravagant stocks. Consider it along these lines: if a $100 stock moves $1, that is a 1% move. In the event that a $5 stock moves $1, that is a 20% move. Numerous new brokers belittle the sort of enthusiastic and monetary harm that this sort of instability can cause. Watcher caution is exhorted.

3. Try not to short stocks

In the event that you are a high-level merchant, do not hesitate to disregard this standard. In the event that you are not, I would truly urge you not to disregard this standard.

To short a stock, you should initially get portions of the stock from your specialist. You at that point sell those offers on the open market. On the off chance that the stock falls in value, you will actually want to repurchase those offers at a lower cost for a benefit.

Assuming, be that as it may, the stock goes up a great deal, you might be compelled to repurchase the offers at a lot greater cost, and wind up losing more cash than you ever had in your exchanging record in any case.

In November 2015, Joe Campbell broke 2 of the 5 precepts. He previously chose to exchange a penny stock called KaloBios Pharmaceuticals. To exacerbate the situation, he chose to short it. At the point when he hit the sack that night, his exchanging account was worth generally $37,000. At the point when he woke up the following morning, the stock had soared. Thus, not just had he lost the entirety of the $37,000, however he currently owed his intermediary an extra $106,000.

What's more, there was no chance to get out. On the off chance that you owe your dealer cash, they can pull you into court and pursue your home and reserve funds. Now and then even the most affluent investors can be cleared out by shorting a stock. During the incomparable Northern Pacific Corner of 1901, portions of that railroad stock went from $170 to $1,000 in a solitary day. That move bankrupted the absolute most well-off Americans of the day, who had shorted the stock and were then compelled to cover at greater costs.

In the event that you do wind up shorting a stock, recollect that your representative will charge you an expense (normally communicated as a yearly financing cost) to acquire the stock. Also, in the event that you are short a stock, you are liable for delivering any profits on that stock (your specialist will naturally remove the cash from your record quarterly).

For these reasons, shorting stocks is obviously a high level and hazardous exchanging procedure. Try not to attempt it until you have been exchanging for in any event 5 years, and you have the monetary soundness to withstand a stunning upwards move in a stock.

Furthermore, never short a penny stock. It is simply not justified, despite the potential benefits.

4. Try not to exchange on edge

To short a stock, you should open up an edge account with your merchant, as Joe Campbell did. You will likewise require an edge account to exchange stocks utilizing edge.

At the point when you purchase a stock on edge, it implies that you are acquiring cash from your intermediary, to buy a bigger number of portions of stock than you would typically have the option to purchase with simply the money sitting in your investment fund.

Suppose that I have $10,000 in my edge account. Most agents in the U.S. will permit me to go on edge to buy $20,000 worth of stock in that account. This means they are loaning me an extra $10,000 (for the most part at some over the top yearly loan cost like 11%, which is the thing that E*TRADE presently charges) to purchase more portions of stock.

In the event that I purchase $10,000 worth of stock and the stock goes up 10%, I've quite recently made $1,000. However, on the off chance that I can build the measure of stock that I'm purchasing to $20,000 utilizing an edge advance, I will have made $2,000 on a similar 10% move. That will imply that my exchanging account has quite recently gone up by 20% ($2,000/$10,000).

Obviously, if the stock goes down 10% and I'm on full edge, I will have lost 20% of my record esteem. Exchanging on edge is accordingly a type of influence: it enhances the exhibition of your portfolio both on the potential gain and the drawback.

At the point when you purchase a stock utilizing edge, the stock and money in your exchanging account are held as security for the edge advance. On the off chance that the stock falls enough, you might be needed to add more money to your record quickly (this is called "getting an edge call"), or danger having the specialist drive you to promptly offer your stock to raise money. Frequently this will prompt your selling the stock at the absolute worst time.

At the point when you open up another investment fund and you are given the decision of a "money account" or an "edge account," it's OK to pick "edge account". An edge account has certain favorable circumstances, for example, having the option to utilize the returns from offering a stock to quickly purchase another stock without trusting that the exchange will settle. In the event that you never surpass your money purchasing influence in an edge account, you won't ever be charged expenses or premium. In that manner, it is very conceivable to have an edge account, however never to go on edge.

Assuming, in any case, you don't confide in yourself, open up a "money account". That way, you won't ever be permitted to exchange on edge.

5. Try not to exchange others' thoughts

The primary explanation never to exchange another person's thoughts is that they presumably don't have the foggiest idea of what they are doing. On the off chance that you get a hot stock tip from your neighbor or at the rec center, it's ideal to overlook it. They likely have no clue about the thing they are discussing. Second, regardless of whether you get a great and genuine exchanging or investing thought from another person, you will presumably not have the conviction to clutch it when difficulties arise. That conviction can just come from building up an exchange thought yourself. At the point when you have planned an exchange, or investigated an investment for yourself, you will have the conviction to hang on. You will likewise know where your stop misfortune is, on the off chance that the stock goes south. Have you seen how hot stock tips never accompanied a suggested stop misfortune level?

Additionally, never place an exchange dependent on something that you have recently perused in Barron's, Forbes, The Wall Street Journal, or have quite recently seen on CNBC. Never purchase a stock dependent on an expert redesign, or sell a stock dependent on an investigator downsize. I have seen investigators at last minimization a stock just whenever it has fallen half. Investigators are slacking markers. They will in general overhaul stocks that have just gone up, and downsize stocks that have just dropped down.

There is likewise a solid choice predisposition among experts. The best experts get employed by mutual funds, and you never get with them again. The most exceedingly terrible investigators stay at the banks or business houses, and keep on administering their unremarkable guidance. Gigantic measures of cash have been lost by following their recommendation. Would it be a good idea for you to try and follow Warren Buffett's recommendation, as I proposed in a past part? Indeed, and no. His recommendation is unquestionably far superior to a hot stock tip from your neighbor. Then again, in the event that you tuned in to him strictly, you passed up the entirety of the incredible tech stocks of the most recent 20 years. He held up until Apple and Amazon were up a huge number of rate focuses before at long last buying them. Anybody can figure out how to think for themselves in the securities exchange, and concoct their own exchanging and investing thoughts. That is the objective behind the entirety of my books and exchanging courses. Instead of giving you a fish, I would much rather show you how to look for yourself. That is the way to genuine independence from the rat race.

Mistakes that even Good Investors had Made

It's not easy to save your money and invest it wisely, especially with economic trends changing all the time. However, there are many pitfalls even for expert investors to avoid that can keep both your wealth and peace of mind intact.

Carelessness

Carelessness is perhaps the most common mistake, and it's usually made when you're fired up by a hot stock tip. This leads to buying and holding onto stocks that are overvalued, or even worse, heavily invested in one single company's shares. You've got to remain rational when investing, and not just focus on how much the company can make you profit. Be realistic about what your expectations will be before getting involved in any investment opportunity.

Overconfidence

Overconfidence is a big danger for those who invest in the stock market independently without any advice or support from experts. The danger stems from the belief that one is smart enough to pick winning stocks without any assistance. Of course, that is impossible—since nobody really knows the future, it is important to pay attention to potential investment opportunities and keep an eye on your investments.

Not Paying Attention to the Company's Condition

A company's assets may be increasing in value and their business may be developing nicely; however, there are some red flags in their current operations that you need to pay attention to. A good example of this is watching the trend of a company's ratio of profit margin versus its asset turnover ratio. If the profit margin remains stable while the asset turnover ratio keeps decreasing or just stays flat then it's an indication that management isn't putting money into research & development for expansion or merger opportunities—a big warning sign.

Lack of Diversification

Many people only invest in the stock market because they want to get rich quick. This is an unwise idea, because greed often leads to investing in only one or two companies that appear to be growing quickly but have nothing behind them. Sure, one or two companies may appear golden right now; however, you need to remain diversified so that if the business fails you won't be left with nothing.

Stock Trading without a Plan

Many people don't have a plan when it comes to investing and just buy stocks on whim and base their decisions off of no information at all. This is a very risky way to invest, as you may end up losing all of your money. When investing, you need to have a solid plan that takes into account the trends of the market and how you will benefit from investing in stocks.

Trying to Time the Market

There is never any surefire way to predict when the stock market will rise or fall, so many investors take this lack of knowledge as an opportunity to make quick money by timing the market. This is dangerous and should be avoided at all costs—if you want to make money in the stock market then do so by investing for the long run and not hoping for short-term gains.

Swing Trading

Some investors get involved in "swing trading"—they buy when the market is low and sell when it rises. This can be a profitable strategy, but only if you are experienced and have a deep understanding of the market. However, it is very risky because if you are wrong even once then you can lose all of your money. Even professional stock traders advise against swing trading, so don't even try it unless you've got lots of practice doing it right.

Keep All Your Eggs in One Basket

This is a very common expression that is often used to describe investing in the stock market. The most common way to put this into practice is by not investing too heavily in any one company, or even worse, investing your life savings into a single company. This can be very risky and it's easy to lose everything if you're not careful.

Watching the Volume

Investors often watch the volume of shares being traded for a certain stock because they want to know how many people are buying and selling stock at any given time. This is a very risky strategy that is difficult to make money off of because the volume of shares related to a company is usually dependent on their growth—if they're not growing then there won't be as many people investing in their stock.

CHAPTER 15. INSIDER'S SECRET OF THE STOCK MARKET

Allow me to begin by helping you to remember quite possibly the main realities about the stock market: *Response to the news is in every case more significant than the actual news.*

Thus, likewise: Response to an income report is in every case more significant than the profit report itself.

It's quite often a bearish sign when a stock auctions after a decent income report. On the off chance that a stock that has had a major run-up falls on a decent profit report, it very well might be an indication that the upturn is finished.

The inverse is likewise obvious. At the point when a stock actually revitalizes after an "awful" profit report, it is a bullish sign. It's additionally a bullish sign if the stock market rallies after a negative financial report.

Numerous individuals get difficult and attempt to guide the stock market. Savvy dealers tune in to the market all things being equal.

Because you need to bring in cash today doesn't imply that the chance will be naturally accessible. You should figure out how to be content with what the market is at present ready to offer you.

Try not to drive an exchange. Be patient, and sit tight for the fat pitch. On the off chance that you can learn persistence and order, the market will at last reward you beyond anything you could ever imagine.

Zero in on a couple of stocks, and become more acquainted with how they exchange. Try not to extend yourself excessively far by attempting to follow such a large number of stocks.

On the off chance that you have committed an error, cut your misfortunes rapidly and proceed onward. Never let an exchange transform into a drawn-out investment. Try not to average exchanging misfortunes. Try not to squander valuable resources. Never add to a losing position, however don't hesitate to add to a position once it begins to bring in cash.

The stock market is a limiting machine. That implies that it takes all accessible data about an organization and the economy and changes a stock's cost in like manner. In some cases it makes a preferable showing of this over different occasions. The stock market tends to over-markdown recognized dangers, and under-rebate unidentified dangers. At whatever point you continue to find out about a danger in the monetary news, it is in all likelihood previously valued into a stock, or the stock market all in all. The dangers you are not hearing anything about, or that appear to be ludicrously far-fetched, that can cause the most harm. In the event that everybody is looking at something, it's quite often as of now estimated into the market. That implies that the stock has just moved to where it should be, founded on the entirety of the data that is as of now accessible. To bring in cash in exchanging or investing, you need to skate to where the puck will be, not to where it has just been.

A market that consistently neglects to move higher will typically go down. The stock market (just as individual stocks) will consistently look out our weaknesses, and move so as to make the most extreme agony the greatest number of merchants.

Temporarily, mass brain science manages the markets, not essentials or the economy. Improving organization essentials and great monetary news will frequently appear in stock costs before they appear in the features, which is the reason it is so imperative to follow through on regard for cost activity.

However long the market is going up, and your stock is going up, don't be in a rush to take benefits. To dominate at this match, you should have a few huge victors. Try not to interfere with them too early.

There is an irregularity to the stock market that we ought not disregard.

Albeit the two most well-known stock market declines both happened in October (1929 and 1987), September has generally been the most fragile month for the stock market. Normal recorded returns for June and August are additionally negative.

This has prompted the renowned articulation "Sell in May and disappear". Stock market gets back from November through April have verifiably been a lot higher than stock market gets back from May through October. This doesn't really imply that you should offer the entirety of your stocks and go to money each May. However, it implies that you ought to be more careful when exchanging throughout the mid-year months. Numerous merchants and investors are at the seashore, so liquidity is lower and instability is higher.

On the off chance that you are searching for a decent long-haul investment, purchase an organization that has the most elevated deals in its industry. So, for home improvement, you need to possess Home Depot; for inexpensive food, McDonald's; for toothpaste, Colgate Palmolive; for installments, Visa; for PDAs, Apple; and for online media, Facebook. When a business sells more than some other organization in its industry, it turns out to be hard to rival. There's not a viable replacement for being #1 in your industry.

At the point when the entirety of the specialists concurs, at that point something other than what's expected will occur in the market. The current customary way of thinking is in every case previously evaluated into the market. Here is a portion of my record-breaking most loved statements about exchanging and the stock market:

- *George Soros:* "It's not whether you're correct or wrong that is significant, but rather how much cash you make when you're correct and the amount you lose when you're off-base."

- *John Maynard Keynes:* "Markets can stay nonsensical longer than you can stay dissolvable."

- *Dennis Gartman*: "The markets will get back to soundness the second that you have been delivered bankrupt."

- *William Eckhardt:* "Either an exchange is sufficient to take, in which case it ought to be actualized at full size, or it's not worth wasting time with by any means."

- *Ed Seykota:* "Basics that you read about are ordinarily pointless as the market has just limited the cost, and I call them 'clever mentals'. I am basically a pattern merchant with bits of hunches dependent on around twenty years of involvement. Arranged by significance to me are: (1) the drawn-out pattern, (2) the current diagram example, and (3) picking a decent spot to purchase or sell. Those are the three essential segments of my exchanging. Path down in far off fourth spot are my crucial thoughts and, very likely, on equilibrium, they have cost me cash."

- *Jim Rogers:* "I simply stand by until there is cash lying in the corner, and I should simply go over yonder and get it. I don't do anything meanwhile. Indeed, even individuals who lose cash in the market say, 'I just lost my cash, presently I need to plan something to make it back.' No, you don't. You ought to stay there until you discover something."

- *Bruce Kovner:* "At whatever point I enter a position, I have a foreordained stop. That is the lone way I can rest. I realize where I'm getting out before I get in. The position size on an exchange is dictated by the stop, and the stop is resolved on a specialized premise."

- *Paul Tudor Jones:* "Don't be a saint. Try not to have a sense of self. Continuously question yourself and your capacity. Never feel that you are excellent. The subsequent you do, you are dead. My greatest hits have consistently come after I have had an incredible period and I began to believe that I knew something."

- *Ed Seykota*: "The way to long haul endure and thrive has a great deal to do with the cash the executives' strategies consolidated into the specialized framework. There are old brokers and there are striking dealers, however there are not many old, intense merchants."

- *Bulls bring in cash, bears bring in cash, however pigs get butchered*. I have heard this old Wall Street maxim very often: it is a warns against greed and impatience of certain investors, represented by the pigs, whose goal is to make the most amount of money in the shortest amount of time. As a result, they tend to lose money, so they get slaughtered.

CHAPTER 16. SOME OF THE TOP TRADERS IN THE STOCK MARKET

Benjamin Graham

Benjamin Graham was born in 1894 in London, United Kingdom. When he was still a child, his family moved to America, where they lost their savings during the 1907 Bank Panic. Graham graduated from Columbia University and began working on Wall Street with Newburger, Henderson and Loeb. At the age of 25, he was already earning around $ 500,000 a year.

In the 1929 stock market crash, Graham lost nearly all of his investments, which taught him some valuable lessons about the world of investing.

His observations after the crash inspired him to write a book with David Dodd, called *"Security Analysis"* first published in 1934, which outlined the fundamental basis of investing in value, which involves buying undervalued stocks. with the potential for growth over time.

According to Graham and Dodd, the investment of value derives from the intrinsic value of an ordinary share independent of its market price. Using factors of a company such as its assets, earnings, and dividend payments, the intrinsic value of a stock can be found and compared with its market value. If the intrinsic value is higher than the current price, the investor should buy and hold until a return to the average occurs. A return to the average is the theory according to which over time the market price and the intrinsic price will converge towards each other until the share price reflects its true value.

In 1949, Graham wrote the famous book *"The Intelligent Investor: The Definitive Book on Value Investing"*, considered the bible of value investing and presents a character known as Mr. Market as a metaphor for the mechanics of market prices.

Graham points out that instead of relying on the daily market sentiments which are driven by the investor's emotions of greed and fear, the investor should perform their own analysis of the value of a stock based on the company's reports on its operations and financial position.

This analysis should reinforce the investor's judgment when he made an offer. According to Graham, the smart investor is the one who sells to the optimists and buys from the pessimists. The investor should look for opportunities to buy low and sell high.

Warren Buffet

With regards to offering monetary guidance, barely any individuals can enthrall a group of people very like Warren Buffet can. His uncommon achievement in the realm of investments—also his $85 billion fortune—implies even those not a tiny smidgen inspired by money sit up and listen when Buffett shares his top tips for accumulating riches.

However Buffett is something beyond the amount of his bank balance (a ten-figure number to be careful). His life is covered in an energy for business and investments and, notwithstanding his tremendous riches, he is broadly known for his liberality and thriftiness—he actually lives in the very home in Omaha in Nebraska that he purchased for $31,000 in 1958 and all the more as of late he has vowed to part with 99% of his abundance to noble cause.

His story is a captivating one without a doubt. Who is Warren Buffet? What is a portion of his rules that you can apply in your life and business? What would you be able to gain from Buffett's own encounters about dealing with your life, cash and vocation?

Buffett has just stood up to and beaten life's difficulties and made a way that could fill in as a triumphant guide for you. You should simply follow that way on your approach to progress. You'll have to change and modify it a little to meet your own circumstances and conditions, however the outline is to a great extent set up. Throughout everyday life and business, you can benefit as much as possible from the intelligence learned by effective and affluent individuals who have made an imprint for themselves around the world and use it as a manual for accomplishing your own objectives.

For quite a long time, Buffett has been a good example to thousands, if not millions, of growing business visionaries and individuals quick to have an effect in their lives.

His prosperity has affected the activities of finance managers all around the planet and has filled in as an uncommon norm to take a stab at both expertly and by and by, gratitude to his liberality and eagerness to help other people.

His impact spreads all over and even those among the most extravagant on the planet have received Buffett's life draws near. Because of Buffett's consolation, for instance, in excess of 160 very rich people have consented to give and part with at any rate half of their abundance for humanitarian causes.

Paul Tudor Jones

Paul Tudor Jones is an American Investor, a mutual funds administrator and he is otherwise called a humanitarian. Jones was brought into the world on September 28th, 1954. His adoration for Hedge store on the board drove him to open his firm back in 1980, an organization by the name Tudor Investment Corporation. The organization's central command is as yet situated in Greenwich, associate cut, and it had some expertise in the administration of resources. Later on, he made Tudor gathering which is a speculative stock investments Holding Company. The Tudor fence organization worked in the administration of fixed pay, monetary standards, values and furthermore products. Throughout the most recent years, his organizations have been doing extraordinary procuring him incredible fortunes since in February 2017, he was assessed to have a net of 4.7 billion by Forbes magazine and this caused him to be number 120 the of the richest individuals on the planet on the class of 400 individuals positioned on the magazine.

Tim Cook

Timothy Donald Cook is the American leader, Industrial Engineer, and Developer. He is at present the Chief boss at the workplaces of Apple Inc. This is the new position he gained at the Apple Inc. since he recently functioned as the Chief Operating Officer under the originator Steve Jobs. Joined Apple in the year 1998 as the senior VP of overall tasks and afterward he later filled in as the chief VP of the world in the division of deals and administrations.

On March 24th, 2011, he was elevated to turn into the Chief leader. He is associated with his dynamic advocating of different mankind and natural development which incorporate the transformation of political of global and nearby observation, online protection, enterprise tax assessment both broadly and universally. Condition's conservation and furthermore the American assembling act.

In the year 2014, Cook became public and recognized himself as gay and was recorded among the 500 CEO at Fortune magazine. Different organizations that Cook worked at incorporate; he was an individual from the leading group of sheets of heads of Nike-Inc., the public football establishment, the trustee of Duke University.

Around 2012, the Apple Inc. organization chose to give Cook a pay of offers worth huge number of dollars vesting in 2016 to 2021. During a public discourse, Cook said that his income from the allowed stocks would be offered to good cause establishments. This incorporates all that he possesses.

George Soros

George Soros is one of the thirty richest men on Earth. He is estimated to have a net worth of $ 25 billion.

Born in Budapest in 1930 to a family of Jewish origin, Soros emigrated to England after surviving the Nazi occupation of Hungary. He graduated from the London School of Economics and then completed a Master in Philosophy.

In 1969, after making his way through various commercial banks, Soros together with Jim Rogers founded the first Double Eagle hedge fund (after renamed Quantum Fund), with a financial endowment of 4 million dollars of capital from investors and 250,000 dollars by way of personal assets.

In 2011, the same fund allowed him to reach $ 25 billion.

Soros is known as the man who got rich by engaging in a series of financial speculations, such as the 1992 short-selling of pounds and lira, which disrupted their respective national governments and banks and earned them billions of dollars.

The concept of reflexivity developed by finance has changed the foundations of the economy. "When markets rise or fall rapidly, they are characterized by imbalances and conventional economic theory does not have to be applied" *he argues.*

In *"The New Paradigm for Financial Markets"* published in May 2008, Soros describes a "super-bubble" that has developed over the previous 25 years and was poised to explode. It was a good prediction: after all, the tycoon never got one wrong.

Carl Icahn

Carl Icahn was brought into the world on Feb 16, 1936, and he is a notable money manager in America. Aside from possessing a few organizations, he was likewise and still most popular for being a sensible investor and givers as well. He established the Icahn Enterprises, and he is the regulator of all the organization's offer since he is the biggest investor. The organization is huge, and it is situated in the New York City. Of late the organization is known as the combination Holding organization, however at first, it was alluded to as American Real bequest Partners. Cahn has additionally led the Federal-Mogul organization, which works in creating, fabricating and furthermore providing the powertrain parts and vehicle security items.

Carl has additionally won hearts of numerous because of his business strategies whereby he was named as the corporate bandit because of his capacity to benefit from the threatening takeover and the resource depriving of the American aircraft. Forbes magazine took a gander at his abundance, and he is assessed to have a sum of 16.6 billion dollars by 2017. He was additionally positioned as number 26 of the most well-off individuals in work on the 400 rich individuals classes. In the support business world, Carl has all the earmarks of being on top five of most well-off men taking the last position.

John C. Bogle

John C. Bogle was born on May 8, 1929, in Montclair, New Jersey to William Yates Bogle Jr. and Josephine Lorraine Hipkins. In 1947 he graduated with honors and was admitted to Princeton University, where he studied economics. During his university years, Bogle studied the mutual fund sector and the link between the cost of a financial product and its profitability: in a sector that was becoming increasingly competitive, being able to do better than the market would always have been more difficult, therefore, it was better to exactly replicate the returns by reducing the difference due to management costs.

In 1951 Walter L. Morgan hired him. In 1970 he replaced Morgan as Wellington's president. He was later fired for an "extremely reckless" merger that he approved.

On May 1, 1975, Bogle founded the Vanguard Company, which is one of the most respected and successful companies in the investment world today.

In 1999 he wrote " *The Little Book of Common Sense on Mutual Funds: New Imperatives for the Intelligent Investor*" which became a classic in the financial community and a best-seller. In the same year, Fortune magazine named Bogle "one of the four investment giants of the twentieth century."

In 2001, he founded the First Index Investment Trust, a precursor to the Vanguard 500 Index Fund, as the first mutual fund available to the general public. The fund replicated the performance of the S&P 500 index and was the first index fund to be sold among retail investors and not just institutional ones. Bogle's innovative idea was to create the first index mutual fund, actually born in 1975. Bogle believed that, instead of beating the index and charging high costs, the index fund would mimic the performance of the index. 'index over the long term, thus achieving higher returns with lower costs than those of actively managed funds. His ideas were so innovative that they led to the founding of the "Bogleheads" movement, a group of individual investors who still today follow the basic principles of his philosophy: start saving when young, diversify, seek simplicity and stay true to their plan. financial regardless of market conditions.

Conclusion

Congratulations for making it to the end. Financial freedom is a long play game in that once you achieve it; you can sit back and enjoy the fruits of your labor. However, before you can reach financial freedom you must first learn to live below your means. This means that for all expenses (not just housing) you spend no more than 60% of your take-home pay. The reason for this is that if an emergency arises, or someone in the family gets sick, or there are other unexpected expenses, then there will be money set aside to take care of these challenges. Next, it is important to determine which expenses are fixed (such as mortgage and utility bills) and which are flexible (such as food and clothing). It is important to practice spending as if everything is flexible except the fixed expenses. It is easy to overspend and ignore the fixed expense portion of your budget, but this can cause a serious cash flow issue as you try to figure out where that money came from. Once you have mastered living below your means and determining fixed expenses, it is time to focus on creating income sources that are not salary-dependent. Many people have these types of accounts but still rely primarily on their salary from their day job for household income. Investing your money for retirement or starting a small business creates an income source that is not salary-dependent. This is important because once you reach retirement age, if you cannot get another job you will be able to live off of the investments you have made for your retirement. Once these two areas are mastered, it is time to create additional sources of income. These may include writing eBooks, selling digital products like online courses, or becoming a consultant for other business owners and professionals. Financial freedom requires that you have multiple streams of income coming in, so that if one area slows down for any reason there are other options that continue to give you an income stream. Don't be fooled... Financial freedom is possible.

If you are still skeptical about the possibility of achieving this goal, here are some quick facts:

- 75% of U.S. citizens are living paycheck to paycheck

- 56% have less than $1,000 in savings, 5% have no savings at all

- 34% of U.S. citizens haven't had a raise in the past five years

- 40 million workers (out of the 120 million) don't have any type of retirement plan set up at their jobs

- 1 out of 5 workers 55 or older say they have no retirement savings or pension

As you can see, there is a definite need to get your financial future moving in the right direction, and it's never too late to turn things around for yourself and your family.

But is financial freedom really possible? Absolutely! There are several key steps to make it happen:

1. Make a list of all your expenses and commitments. This will help you figure out where you're spending your money, how much you have left over, and where you can cut back. Once the numbers are in front of you, see if there is anything that can be cut back or eliminated altogether. Only after taking a hard look at your situation will you be able to figure out any ways that may help save some money or get yourself in a better financial position.

2. Use the "Pay Yourself First" Principle to Budget Your Money. Pay yourself first by putting money away before you pay your bills or take care of your other financial commitments. The idea is to put a portion of the money you make into an "emergency fund" and/or retirement account. This way, if something comes up unexpectedly, you don't have to worry about paying for it on credit or dipping into your savings. You have already taken care of it ahead of time.

3. Avoid debt as soon as possible. If there are any debts that you carry around from month-to-month, start attacking those first in order to get them out of the way faster (and to avoid interest charges). The longer you let debt go, the more expensive it gets.

4. Start putting money into your retirement account. One of the best ways to begin is to start up a Roth IRA (Roth Individual Retirement Account). With a Roth IRA, you can withdraw money without having to pay any penalties or interest on it if you need it for certain expenses (such as college tuition). You'll also have the freedom to use that money whenever and however you wish in retirement (since by then it will be yours!).

5. Remember that successful saving depends on your buying power, not the number of years you work. A person who begins saving at age 25 (with a 5% savings rate) will have 50% more purchasing power than someone who waits until age 35 to save.

6. Don't be afraid to take risks. Let's face it—no matter how much money you might make, there are times when you just don't have any left over each month after all your bills and other financial commitments are taken care of. If this is just like your situation, you need to start thinking outside the box, and that means taking some calculated risks. Start investing in income-producing real estate (even if it's just a modest investment) or start your own business. The rewards can be great, but only if you take the risk!

7. Don't give up! If you don't see results in the beginning, don't give up! Give yourself some time to make things happen and keep working towards your goal.

In order to achieve financial freedom, you have to stop blaming others for your problems and start taking responsibility for your own life. Commit yourself to your ultimate goal of achieving financial freedom, and you'll be one step closer to achieving your dreams!

Risks of Not Investing

You Don't Have a Plan

If you don't have an investment plan in place, you are really just guessing about where you think your money will be in the future. Why not take a bit of time to figure out what's important to you now and determine how long you would like your money to last?

You're Lacking Long-Term Goals

If there are no big goals in your life, then there is also no need for long-term planning and investing. Luckily, you have time, but setting out some goals today is a great way to keep your motivation up and give yourself a clear vision of what your future looks like.

The Downside of Investing

Investing in the stock market can be terrifying, there is no doubt about that. If you start taking a look at the past performance of the stock market and see some really bad years, it can certainly make you wary of making investments today. Don't let this get to you—stocks have more good years than they do bad; historically speaking (according to Yale University). From 1871-2014, the average annualized return on stocks was 7%.

Wall Street

If you are hesitant about investing in the stock market because you do not understand Wall Street, then this is another reason why you need to take some time to learn more about how it works.

You're Too Afraid to Invest

This may sound silly, but some people are too afraid to invest because they think it will cost too much or take too much work. There is an old saying that goes something like *"you miss 100% of the shots you never take".* If you're looking for more information, we recommend checking out this post from Carl Richards that outlines all the reasons you're too afraid to invest.

You Don't Have a Plan B

Having a plan is important, but even more important 0is knowing what will happen if your plan doesn't work out. Having an investment plan in place is great, but if something happens and your investments drop dramatically, it's good to have some sort of backup plan so that you can adjust accordingly. This could mean laying out another investment plan with new goals or cutting back on your spending until your portfolio recovers.

You Think It's Too Complicated

If you are worried about the intricacies of the market, don't be. Investing is actually quite simple if you just start with a few basic steps. As you gain more confidence and momentum, you can add additional investments to your portfolio, but it is important to start small and work your way up to larger portfolios over time.

You Don't Have the Time

This is another misconception that some people have about investing: that it takes too much time or that they don't have enough time for all their other responsibilities and commitments in life. If you are working more than 40 hours a week, then you've got some extra time to devote to investing. It's important to make the time, especially if you are trying to build wealth and save for your future.

You Lack Control

If you are averse to investing because you feel like your money is just going into some black hole and there is nothing that can be done about it, then this is another misconception that needs to be cleared up. Investing in the stock market will give you more control than any other investment vehicle out there—if something goes wrong with one of your stocks or funds, then it will correct over time and you can sell it at a profit (or loss).

You're Afraid to Make an Investment Mistake

This is another big fear that keeps people from investing: that they will make a mistake and lose all their money. This is not very likely if you are using an investment professional or do some sort of due diligence on your own before you invest.

Introduction

We can't even count the number of young adults who have at one time or another watched a TV show about entrepreneurship or read a magazine article claiming that they can be rich too, by investing wisely in stocks.

The idea is appealing to anyone who wants to take control of their future and life decisions, because it suggests that money doesn't matter as much as getting the right investment decisions. Unfortunately, this kind of thinking is dangerous. Not only does it typically take decades for most investors to "get it right"—if they ever do—but there's also no guarantee that your teen will want the same things in 20 years that he or she wants today.

The fact is that for most young people, investing might not be the most important thing in their lives. Until they get older and established in a career, saving and investing for retirement may not be at the top of their priority list; there are other things that might seem more pressing and exciting at this stage in life.

When you're young, you have limited resources to invest. You're also still trying to figure out who you are—what kind of career or education you want to pursue, and how much risk you want to take with your money. For these reasons, it's not a good idea to jump into the stock market before you have a better handle on your financial circumstances and goals.

This doesn't mean you'll never be able to invest in the stock market, but it does mean that you're a long way off from making a decision that will have a major impact on your life. Until then, there are plenty of other ways to get started with investing and the stock market without getting ahead of yourself.

The Basics of Stock Market Investing

To understand how stocks work, you first need to know what stocks actually represent. A company's stock represents a portion of the company's ownership—or equity in it. Think of it as a loan to the company—you are lending them money, and they promise to pay that money back with interest, as well as give you part of the profits from any growth in their business. If you want to buy stock in a company and receive those potential profits, then you must first purchase shares. For now, it's important to know that stock market investing is simply the process of purchasing shares of stock. Of course, knowing what stocks represent isn't enough—you also need to know how stocks actually work. They can be volatile—and that means that they go up and down in value over time. The simplest way to think about stock market investing is to imagine a roller coaster: the prices climb higher as demand increases. And then, at some point, they drop precipitously; this is called a crash. If you're going to invest in stocks, then you have to be prepared for price fluctuations like these. If you buy at the high of the roller coaster and sell at the low, then it doesn't make sense to call yourself an "investor" because you aren't investing—you're speculating. And this kind of behavior can be extremely dangerous.

CHAPTER 1. INVESTING: WHY?

No matter what your age is, it's important to have a bit of money stashed away. And as you're only getting older, the principle only gains even more importance. Why? Well, because if you don't have any money saved up for retirement yet, or even just enough to get by and not depend on others for financial assistance in case you ever need it in the future then you've got some serious thinking ahead of you. This is why.

To start things off, it's important to understand what investing is and why it's an important topic for everyone you know, whether they're teens or seniors. Investing isn't just about money—it's about planning for your future. Investing is the practice of putting your money into some kind of investment that will eventually pay off some sort of financial benefit in the future. In other words, it's a way to make more money while waiting for the time when you'll need it at a later point in your life.

So why is investing important? Well, for one thing, it's the kind of thing that can help you do things in the future if you don't have much money in your pocket right now. Many people start investing because they want to buy a house, buy a car, or pay for their children's university education in the future. Others use it as a way to secure their retirement and avoid becoming dependent on others for financial aid. Whatever the reason may be for you personally, investing is almost always an essential part of planning your financial future. Of course, when you're young, it can be pretty easy to think that investing is only for those who have a lot of money to spare. The point of investing isn't necessarily about the amount of money you've got in your pocket—it's about being smart with your finances and putting some money away for the future when you'll need it.

So if you're worried about having enough money for retirement someday, then starting to invest now can help take care of things for you down the line. But even if you're just looking to save a bit of money while you're still young, investing can still help you out. In fact, one of the greatest things about investing is that it helps protect your money so that it can't be lost so easily. What does this mean? Well, with investing, you have more control over where and how your money is spent. For instance, instead of having to buy something expensive today and then paying for it over time (as in the case of credit cards or loans), your investment lets you pay off the obligation gradually so that you don't have to make such a big investment all at once.

Investing may sound like a daunting prospect, but it doesn't have to be. It's actually very simple and straightforward—you put your money into stocks, bonds, mutual funds or even real estate in order to earn money from the interest or profit these investments generate.

The earlier you start investing for your future, the better off you will be as an adult. The sooner you start saving and investing, the less risk there is that one day your egg nest will be significantly smaller than it would have been if you had started saving and investing when you were younger.

If you're wondering how old you have to be to start investing, we've got the answer. First off, it depends on the type of investment: stocks and bonds can both be traded by people 18 and up, while most retirement accounts and IRAs require that you reach a certain age or birthday before you can participate (things like social security). Some savings account also have minimum age requirements—for instance, most savings account for children usually involve parental consent until they reach a certain age. So, when is your birthday? Oh! It's coming up in just one week? Great! In this case, you'll need to wait 12 more months (365 days) before your first withdrawal from retirement fund is allowed. But don't lose hope! You'll be eligible to start investing in stocks, bonds, IRAs and other savings plan once you reach 18 years old.

To help put things into perspective, the average American household headed by someone between 31–35 years old has only $6k saved for retirement. With that in mind, it's clear that many people are having trouble saving enough for retirement on their own—it's been reported that many people end up retiring significantly under the poverty line. That's why it pays to start as early as possible! By starting at a young age, you don't have to worry about being able to save up enough money later on down the line. But not all investment accounts are created equal. Some investments require you to be a certain age to participate, while others may be opened up for anyone to join.

Many parents may be reluctant to teach their kids about finances, but the sooner this responsibility is taken on, the better off your child will be for it. Learning about money and investing early in life will put your child in a better position to start saving for retirement while they are still young. Knowledge of personal finance can help your child become aware of the skills necessary to manage money more efficiently throughout their lifetime and it could help them avoid common missteps among young adults today like living paycheck-to-paycheck or accumulating high levels of debt.

Start Early

When your child is very young, instill in them the importance of saving for the future. Help them to develop a sense of responsibility at an early age by teaching them something as simple as how to open a savings account or start contributing to their college fund. Keep this up as they grow older, and even reinforce the importance of investing when they are just starting off on their own. Children who start young and invest consistently have the best shot at achieving financial security in the long-term.

Tie It into Life Lessons

The best way to get kids interested in personal finance is to make it a priority when you're teaching them other life lessons. For example, if you're struggling with your child to get them to save their allowance, try tying it into a lesson about budgeting. When you allow your children to buy something with their allowance, be sure they know how much money is left in their account. You can even start by explaining how you use budgeting and saving strategies yourself.

Teaching kids about investing when they are young may seem daunting but spending time with them and being an example for them is a great way to help them learn the value of starting early and sticking with it.

Teens are faced with many challenges, and being able to face them head-on is crucial. There isn't a better way to do that than by teaching them about investing.

Investing allows teens to take control of their own finances. Investing can help a teen start making smart decisions early on in life, and hopefully avoid crippling debt later on.

Investing also teaches teens about delayed gratification, the ability to work towards and accomplish long-term goals—a skill that will carry over into their future relationships with others as well as themselves. In addition to these more obvious skills, investing can also teach teens about personal responsibility. It allows them to experience failures, set their own goals, and work towards making those goals a reality. By teaching teens about investing early on, they can prepare themselves for challenges that inevitably await them in the future.

Teaching teens about investing is also beneficial because it teaches them to create opportunities for themselves rather than waiting for others to create them for them. A popular example of this is the popularity of "influencers" made famous by Jonah Berger's book Contagious. These are teens and young adults who actively seek out sponsorships from brands in order to create their own income streams. This is huge for two reasons. One, it teaches teens to be proactive about their financial future rather than waiting for opportunities to come to them. Two, it teaches them the importance of strategic marketing—because they have no money being put into their business, they have to find ways to market themselves in a strategic manner that produces results.

These are skills that will help teens avoid the debt that so many in their generation seem destined for. By teaching teens about investing early on, they can avoid the pitfalls of debt and instead create opportunities for themselves throughout life. Achieving Financial Freedom and wealth requires determination, patience, and consistency. More than anything else, you have to be able to delay gratification and stay on the path. You have to be courteous with your resources. If you want Financial Freedom, it is going to take time. It's not something you can buy or happen overnight. Financial Freedom is built over a long time. Many young people today have not learned how to delay gratification. They expect to have everything they want in life, and they want it now! This is a major reason why they get into debt so easily and live paycheck-to-paycheck. Do you see yourself in this profile? If so, it's time to change your mindset. Stop living on credit and start living within your means. You CAN find ways to save money while you're working hard toward Financial Freedom. You just have to look for them and be willing to make adjustments in your life, especially in the way you spend.

People who approach building wealth differently by valuing Financial Freedom know that it requires sacrifice. They have the discipline to put off buying things they want today so that they can buy freedom later on. The key is to learn how to be happy with what you have right now, not focusing on what you don't have or what you can't afford. You have to be more thoughtful, and you have to be willing to accept less in the short-term so that you can have greater abundance in the long run.

If you dig into the wealthiest people's past, you'll find that they were usually not born rich. They had to start from scratch just like everyone else; however, they made a decision at some point that working hard was not enough. They determined that they wanted Financial Freedom and wealth as well, eventually breaking free from the cycle of working for money-paying bills-working for more money-paying more bills—and never getting ahead. This is the classic rat race.

Knowing that they wanted Financial Freedom, these people began to make different choices in their lives. They learned to control their spending, saving and investing on a regular basis. Yes, it was a struggle at first, but after getting through the initial hardship, they created an easier lifestyle for themselves over time. They did whatever it took to get ahead and to achieve their dreams of Financial Freedom. As they became more successful, the more they could live life how they really wanted.

CHAPTER 2. GETTING AND MANAGING MONEY

Step-By-Step Guide to Create a Basic Balance Sheet with Excel

Step 1:

Regardless, compose the title of your financial record. The chief line is the association's name, second line is "asset report" and third line is the finish of the enterprise's accounting time period (as picture shows). From here on out, you need to discover assets and add them into four classes on the left side: current asset, long term asset, intangible asset and other asset.

Finally, figure the total sum of each part and notwithstanding them together to get the total asset number.

Step 2:

Register each asset class and add them together.

1. Absolute current assets= cash + accounts receivable + Inventory + prepaid security

2. Hard and fast long stretch asset = investments + buildings + gear gathered crumbling

3. Complete unimportant assets = goodwill + licenses

Hard and fast assets = Total current assets + Total long stretch liabilities + Total elusive assets.

Step 3:

Gap liabilities into current liabilities and long stretch liabilities. Once-over each and every current risk (bank liabilities, compensation payable, premium payable, messages payable) and long stretch liabilities (notes payable, securities payable) autonomously in a segment.

Step 4:

Process the all-out current liabilities and long-haul liabilities and add them together.

1. Total current liabilities = accounts payable + compensation payable + interest payable + charges payable

2. All out long-haul liabilities = notes payable + bonds payable

All out liabilities = Total current liabilities + Total long-haul liabilities.

Step 5:

Overview all the stockholders' equity record and process the complete number.

Step 6:

Gather Liabilities and Stockholder's record into a single unit to get the sum comparable to add up to assets.

Here is a picture of a sample balance sheet of a company:

Setting and Reaching Short-Term Goals (Buy a Videogame) and Long-Term Goals (Buy a PlayStation)

We all want to reach our goals, but it's sometimes difficult to set and stick with them. They feel daunting. But the truth is that small goals are more manageable and help you motivate yourself to continue taking steps forward. I will outline how I've been able to set achievable short-term goals (such as buying a videogame) and long-term goal (such as buying a PlayStation).

Short-Term Goals can be outlined in the form of:

"I will buy a videogame by next Friday" or "I will save $200 dollars by next Thursday." Long-Term Goals can be defined as: "I will buy my own PlayStation by April 2020."

I will do this by:

"I will save $200 by next Thursday."

I am able to set these goals by writing them down on a sheet of paper and crossing them out as I achieve them. This helps me feel accomplished and rewarded. It also helps me realize that I'm actually able to accomplish the goal, since it's in front of me.

If you want to achieve your long-term or short-term goal, you must first realize that it is possible. You must believe in yourself. If you don't believe you can do it, then why would anyone else?

Next, you must set up a game plan. What are the steps that you will take to reach your goal? This is where writing things down comes in handy. When I set a goal, I write my steps, step by step and create an action plan and timeline for reaching them.

Once the game plan is made, it will be easier to stick to it. You should also look for ways to motivate yourself along the way—this can be anything from buying a new book about your goal to going out for ice-cream after hitting your daily step count. It's important to also think about how you're going to reach your goals in the first place. If you want to lose weight, exercise is an obvious solution. If you want to save money, putting more of your income into savings or investments is a good idea. Whatever way you choose to reach your goal, it will help if you put a bit of time into planning how you'll get there. Remember that setting small goals and achieving them will push you toward the larger one. For example, if my goal is to improve my running times by 10 % over the next 6 months. But first I will set a 1000-meter race (220 yards) to run in 90 seconds. Then I will set 905 meters (3 quarters of a mile) to run in 90 seconds. This will eventually lead to running a 3000-meter race (1 mile) in 2 minutes 20 seconds.

The idea here is that I achieve sprints (small goals) on the way to achieving bigger goals. This is a good way to set goals because it gives you a sense of stability and makes you feel confident that you can accomplish your big goal.

How to Earn Your Own Money and Increase Your Goals-Budget

There is a wide range of ways wherein you can bring in your own cash.

The first "way" is called "pocket money." It's the point at which a grown-up gives a kid a specific measure of cash every week, usually between $5-10 AUD (Australian Dollars). Sometimes it tends to be pretty much than this relying upon how much the parent earns and the age of the youngster. The parent gives the youngster the money every week, usually on a Friday or Saturday. The child can spend it anyway they like, however they must be honest. It's sometimes called "remittance." You can also "win" or get money from others like relatives, yet this is less basic than pocket money. On the off chance that you bring in your own cash—and if it's for your own goals—it's easier to contact them because you don't need to ask others for your money.

The second "way" is called gifts from relatives (like parents or grandparents). This happens when a grown-up gives a youngster some cash either for a special occasion or just something that occurred in their life (like getting passing marks at school). Gifts from relatives is similar to pocket money, however it's usually given for a special occasion in the youngster's life such as a graduation, birthday or Christmas. The third "way" is known as a summer job. This is the point at which a grown-up gives a young person (usually 14–17 years old) some cash every week as well as some additional things like mid-day breaks and available time. It's known as a "summer job" because it usually happens throughout the summer before secondary school or university. The money is mostly spent on different things, however it tends to be used to arrive at goals.

Where to Put Your Money: Piggy Bank Vs. Money Account

Would you put your money in a piggy bank or deposit it into a bank account? What are the pros and cons of both options? Here we will discuss the benefits and pitfalls of both, so you can decide for yourself. Piggy banks are brightly colored containers that hold coins and cash. These containers come in many shapes, with collectible items like Star Wars characters or Disney princesses on them. The problem with piggy banks is that they're not insured—if they get lost, broken, or stolen there's no refund.

In contrast to a free piggy bank account is an actual saving account at a financial institute like TD Canada Trust. These accounts come with a number of benefits, including safety and protection against theft.

The Benefits of Piggy Banks

Piggy banks are ideal for children learning to save, as they are easy to use and allow kids to see their money grow. Piggy banks are also a great way to teach your kids that saving is important and that they can earn interest on their money by keeping it in the bank—even if it's a piggy bank!

The Downside of Piggy Banks

The main problem with piggy banks is that no matter how cute they look, cash and coins left in them will simply sit there, not earning any interest. That's because piggy banks aren't insured or regulated like banks are. This means that there's no free insurance if your bank gets lost or stolen.

The Benefits of a Money Account

A money account is a financial safety net that lets you make deposits and withdrawals at any time. This means that your money is insured by the government if you deposit it in an account at a bank or financial institute (like TD Canada Trust)—so it's protected from theft.

You can also open up savings accounts for your children. This way, you can deposit money into their accounts to teach them about saving while still protecting their money from them. That way, when they want to buy something, they'll be limited to the amount of money in their account, and won't have access to any more cash than that.

The Downside of Money Accounts

Money accounts are great for peace of mind—who wouldn't like to know that their cash is protected? However, savings accounts typically don't earn much interest at all—not enough to make it worth depositing money into them for any real length of time. The interest rates for savings accounts are so low that it's not worth keeping money in a savings account—you'll be better off if you keep your money in your chequing account.

Savings Account Teen-Friendly

A teen-friendly savings account is one that has:

- **Low fees:** It's important not to overpay on fees because the money saved will add up to a significant sum of money. For example, if you bank with Chase and are charged $4 for using a non-Chase ATM, you'll pay $96 in ATM fee charges per year, which would have grown to over $5000 had it been invested conservatively. And don't forget about overdraft protection fees!

- **No monthly minimum:** You shouldn't be penalized for not having much money to save because of having a high minimum balance.

- **Access to ATMs:** In order to avoid fees and keep your balance accessible, choose a bank that has an ATM network or allows you to use other banks' ATMs. And if possible, choose an account that lets you withdraw cash from a teller for free.

Tip: With the exception of the account at First National Bank, all accounts in this table charge monthly fees unless you maintain a sufficient balance to waive them. If possible (depending on how much money is available), pick a savings account with no minimum balance requirement and low or no fees.

CHAPTER 3. BUSINESS AND FINANCIAL CONCEPTS

We will explore what business and financial concepts are, how they make the world of investments work, and what you can do to apply this knowledge in your own life. Business and financial concepts are broad areas of study with a range of sub-fields. These include accounting, finance, economics, law & ethics, marketing, management & leadership, organizational behavior and sociology.

There is no single definition for "business" or "financial concept," but both can be generally defined as systematic attempts to make money through selling goods or services for profit.

In the broadest sense, a good or service is something that people are willing to pay for. A bus driver obviously needs to make money, but they often get paid for driving (and associated time and energy) rather than by selling a product or service.

A factory worker who is paid an hourly wage will receive minimal money depending on how much work they do, but in many cases won't be expected to sell anything at all.

The concept of "value" comes into play here as well: if workers were only paid based on how much value their efforts produced, then a worker who produced twice the goods as another would potentially earn twice as much pay. As a result, many employers pay employees on an hourly basis which is then divided by the number of hours worked to get an effective hourly rate.

This is then adjusted by adding on a fixed amount to get a total take-home wage which may include "extras" like health insurance or retirement benefits.

In this example, the worker contributes their time and energy to producing goods or services that are in demand. The employer in turn sells these goods or services for a profit.

As long as both parties see value in the exchange, it will continue to happen.

One important note about market value is that its relative nature means that what is valuable to one person may not be valuable to another. For example, due to higher wages, food service workers in the United States have a greater purchasing power than agricultural workers in India. The agricultural worker will value rice more than the American worker because they have less money to spend and rice fills their daily nutritional requirements.

In a similar way, an investment manager who works 80 hours per week may only be able to afford $20 worth of groceries whereas an idle housewife may easily spend $200 on a shopping spree. This relative value is called "opportunity cost" and it has important implications for investment. We'll discuss opportunity cost more in a future post.

One of the essential things that separates people from animals is the ability to think and make decisions. For instance, if you were starving and someone handed you a slice of pizza, you could eat it. If you were given an entire pizza and told that it was poisoned, you would likely avoid eating it, even though it is literally the same amount of food as before.

This process of analyzing and making decisions based on information that we've gathered is referred to as critical thinking. As you can see, it's an important skill when it comes to business and finance because it helps us make the right decisions about what to invest in and how much money to risk.

In addition, decision-making skills are important for entrepreneurs who must weigh important variables when deciding what kind of business or product to start. For example, if your great idea is a hamburger stand with $5 burgers, that's not going to be a successful business in some parts of the world where people have less money.

At the same time, if you choose to start a $5,000-per-plate restaurant you'd better make sure you're able to get enough customers to earn your investment back and more.

Human communities have been upholding laws for as long as we've been around. Laws are important because they regulate behavior and ensure that people can live and work together in an orderly way. Without these rules we'd have chaos! Of course this doesn't mean that there aren't situations where rules or laws are broken, but many of them exist for a reason.

Businesses have similar rules: they must abide by the law in every country that they do business in. In addition, they must follow both internal company policies and government regulations. These rules help ensure the long-term viability of organizations by making sure that they don't lose money through illegal or unsafe business practices.

Financial concepts are all around us, influencing our decisions every day. The course of history has been shaped by powerful people making good financial decisions, and ruined by those who made bad ones.

For example, if the Roman emperor Caligula had made better financial choices early in his reign, he might have avoided bankruptcy and a brutal assassination at the hands of rivals jealous of his power.

On a more positive note, the financial decisions of the leaders of the United States have helped to create one of the world's largest and most prosperous economies. Financial intelligence involves using our knowledge to make smart decisions and solve problems when they arise. It also gives us tools we can use to plan for all aspects of our lives, both current and future.

In particular, financial intelligence helps us make smart investments that will help us reach our long-term goals and dreams.

The Power of Compounding Interest

Compound interest is a form of interest that accumulates and results in earnings on earnings. Compound interest can be thought of as "interest on interest."Let's make a distinction immediately: simple or compound interest? Simple interest is the one defined above, while compound interest is interest on interest. We contextualize simple interest and compound interest both in the world of financial investments, which is what interests us specifically. Simple interest is the return that is paid to you consistently, based on an initial invested capital, which does not increase because you periodically withdraw the earnings.

I'll give you a concrete example.

Invest a sum of $20,000 in an instrument with which you earn 10% per annum, you will find yourself a sum of $22,000 at the end of the year; subsequently withdraw the $2,000 of profit and repeat the same investment with the initial capital always of $20,000. After 10 years, you will find yourself $40,000, or you will have doubled the initial capital. Compound interest, on the other hand, is based on the continuous reinvestment of the accumulated earnings, without the withdrawal at the end of the year.

Take the same example again but, after earning $2,000 in the first year, invest the total accumulated capital in the second year, i.e. the sum of $22,000 and not $20,000 as in the first example. The initial invested capital will gradually increase after each year and therefore the annual earnings will increase accordingly. In this second case, after 10 years you will earn $51,875. In the image below you can see what happens in the two cases of simple interest and compound interest.

Do you understand the importance of compound interest and why do you have to use it to earn over time? The principle of compound growth has been around for centuries, but the term "compound interest" was first used by Albert Einstein in 1921. Today we owe much of our economic success to the use of compound liability as a means for banks and pension funds to generate income through investments.

In summary, compounding allows you to earn money with some level of safety on your principal investment and it is not just an abstract mathematical theory—it happens every day.

Compound interest formula: $A=P(1+r)\ n$

Where: P=Principal; r=Annual Rate; n=time period in years.

In the image below we can get a visual idea of how compound interest works.

CHAPTER 4. THE STOCK MARKET

Primary and Secondary Market

The Difference Between Primary Stock Markets and Secondary Stock Markets: The primary markets are—as the name suggests—the first buyer-seller interaction, where brokers buy shares from their clients to sell on to another client. It's worth noting that this only applies to publicly traded companies. Secondary markets are where individual investors or non-brokerage firms trade with each other through privately negotiated transactions. Both the primary and secondary markets are for existing stock. When a company sells out for a new product or service, they do so by issuing new shares. When this happens, you'll have a primary market to buy them and if the company is successful, then you'll have a secondary market to sell them on. However, it's worth noting that this doesn't always happen as things can get complicated (even more than they already are).

Primary markets are an important part of bringing new capital to firms looking for funding from investors to expand. So if you want to invest in stocks, it's likely that you're going to have to start with the primary markets before venturing into secondary markets.

How It All Works

If you're still confused about how primary and secondary markets work, here's more information.

Assuming we're looking at the stock market from an individual point of view, you're going to want to invest in a company. So let's say you've decided to invest in Facebook, which was founded in 2004 by Mark Zuckerberg. Before that happened, Facebook needed funding and they got it from venture capitalists (VCs) like Benchmark Capital and Greylock Partners. Once they had the funding, Facebook was free to expand—but they were still backed by VCs.

As Facebook's popularity grew, secondary markets emerged where people could buy and sell shares in the company. This is how you can invest in stock markets—it's a representation of the underlying value of a company. If Facebook was to sell 100 million shares, they'd have to split them up somehow among investors or they'd lose value. The value translates directly from the company share value—if you wanted to buy 10% of Facebook, then that's how many shares you'd have to purchase (and that would severely hurt your pocket).

Facebook isn't listed on the New York Stock Exchange (NYS-E) yet—it lists on NASDAQ instead. There's a lot of technical information behind this, but the main difference is that NASDAQ is a quasi-private market, which means it isn't run by investors—it's run by the NASDAQ hierarchy. It also has different rules than NYS-E, so if Facebook were to list on NYSE down the line, they'd have to adhere to their rules and regulations.

So you decide you want to get in on the action and buy Facebook shares—what happens next? Do you have a broker who handles your transactions for you? Well most people don't deal directly with brokers—these trades are usually made through mutual funds, which are generally cheaper. Mutual funds are a "collection of stocks" usually managed by a seasoned broker and you can invest in it through them. Mutual funds aren't a bad idea for beginners, but you'll probably eventually move on to individualized stock picking—if you feel confident enough to do so.

So now you've bought your Facebook shares through a mutual fund—what happens next? Do they arrive as physical pieces of paper or do they just get added to your account? Well the latter is true—most transactions are done electronically these days. You'll have to check with your broker to see how they prefer to receive your trade, but it's likely that you'll have to provide them with your bank details and the broker will make a deposit into your account. You can also buy physical shares—these are worth more because there's a limit on how many you can hold, so they sell for a premium.When you decide to sell, the same thing happens in reverse. You contact the mutual fund and let them know how many shares you wish to sell and then they do the rest. Once the transaction has been made, you'll receive the money from the sale in your bank account in a matter of days. So how do you make money? The first way is through dividends—if you own stocks, then you can likely receive a dividend. If Facebook decided to give its shareholders $0.50 per share, then those who invested $100 would receive $5 (depending on the price of their shares). Some stocks pay more dividends than others, but it's usually on a quarterly basis.

The second way to make money is to sell your shares for more than you bought them for. This is called a capital gain. So if you bought $100 worth of Facebook shares in 2010 and sold them in 2012, but they increased by $10, then you made a $10 capital gain—which is nice.

Market's Rules

The rules of the stock market do not apply to these individuals. They apply only to smaller investors like you and me. And even though these rules do not change our probability of success, they do change our expectancy from investing in stocks. In other words, following these rules can increase your chances for profit over time by reducing your risk as an investor.

Below are the most important rules you should understand about investing in stocks:

1) The Stock Market is a zero-sum game. This means that for every winner there must be another loser. It's important to note that the players in this game aren't necessarily human, but rather institutions like banks and brokerages.

2) The Market knows more than you do and anticipates your actions. Don't rely on information from other investors or news channels to make decisions about investing in stocks. Instead, rely on your own analysis of company fundamentals, valuations, and macroeconomic factors to make decisions.

3) The Market is highly efficient. This means that no matter how much analysis you do, it will be difficult to beat the market consistently over time. This efficiency explains why index funds have outperformed many mutual funds over the past 10 years. Therefore, your investing strategy should focus on minimizing risk and understanding when to exit stocks, not trying to beat the market.

4) Stock Prices can go down as well as up. There are always two sides of a coin and that's true with stocks as well. Therefore, don't get too excited about raising a stock price more than 25% from its long-term average or you could get burned (see Cramer's Rule).

5) Be an Accumulator. If you intend to save for retirement or spend the money you've accumulated over time, don't expect your stocks to go up more than 25% a year. This will allow you to average out losses and enjoy consistent gains.

Concepts of Risk and Volatility

Risks are potential losses that may or may not occur, and they are the reason we take steps to lessen our exposure to them. Volatility is the magnitude of price changes in financial markets. Together, these concepts form a powerful combination for investors. So what does this mean? Let's break it down.

Risks: Potential losses that may or may not occur depending on future events.

Volatility: The magnitude of price changes in financial markets often represented by the percentage of change over time or standard deviation from a moving average.

Together—Powerful combo for investors: Risk and volatility together can give investors more information on market behavior which they can use to make better decisions when managing their portfolios.

Since risk and volatility are important components for investors to be aware of, we will take a deeper look at these topics, including what each is and how each can be calculated.

Risk: Risks are potential losses that may or may not occur depending on future events. Risk is a forward-looking concept that can be seen as uncertainty of future price or rate of return.

Volatility: Volatility is the magnitude of price changes in financial markets. Volatility is often represented by the percentage of change over time or standard deviation from a moving average. Currency volatility can also be represented in terms of foreign exchange rates between two currencies.

The time horizon for volatility depends on the financial instrument being analyzed. For example, stock volatility may be calculated by day, month, quarter or year while bond volatility may be calculated by maturity or duration. The time horizon for risk depends on the type of risk being evaluated and must allow enough time to adequately estimate future losses.

Stock Market Indexes

What Is an Index?

An index is a portfolio comprised of many securities that represent a market or an industry sector. The most popularly known indices are the Dow Jones Industrial Average (DJIA), NASDAQ, and S&P 500... but there are many other types of indices. For example:

- The Russell 2000 is an index of smaller companies in the US,

- The FTSE 250 is a UK index of mid-cap companies, and
- The Hang Seng Index is Hong Kong's stock market index.

Index funds have a few advantages over individual securities. For one, since index funds buy many stocks at once, they can buy more shares at lower costs.

Warren Buffet often talks about the power of compound interest—this means that if you invest $100 at 7% for 10 years, you will not just have $107 when you're done but rather $219.8. Index funds allow an investor to lock in market returns over long periods of time for far less money and time than it would take to work with individual stocks and still get a similar result! Indexing is a way to invest in the stock market without paying fees to a professional money manager.

Bull and Bear Market

While stocks values have risen generally since the early 22nd century, we have seen periods of declining stock prices and periods when they were flat. When the value of stocks declines markedly in a comparatively short period of time, it is known as a "bear market." The term "bear market" was coined by Charles Dow during the Wall Street Crash of 1907.

A bear market is often part of an economic recession or depression (although not always), and typically ends with strong price increases once the economy recovers.

A bull market is a market that's doing well. The term comes from the image of crowds of people conniving to purchase stocks, pushing the prices higher and higher. A bear market is a stock market where share prices are falling.

A bull market can be seen in the long-term view as one of four phases in an economic expansionary period or as part of a supercycle; likewise, a bear market can be seen in relation to an economic recession or as part of a correction after a supercycle has ended.

Historically, a bear market coincided with the crash. But, in modern times, stocks recovered quickly from the latter event and went on to make new highs.

CHAPTER 5. UNDERSTANDING STOCKS

Types of Stocks and Their Classification

It is much easier to invest in stocks if you know how different types of stocks are classified. Not only does this help you understand things simpler, but it also helps you to find the right investments for your portfolio. Here are three major classifications of stocks and how they can be identified:

- **Small-Cap:** The stock market defines small-cap as stocks that have a total market capitalization below $1 billion (around). These companies tend to be on the lower side of the spectrum in terms of complexity and stability, meaning that they're higher risk with lower returns on average for investors looking for these traits in their investment opportunities.

- **Large-Cap**: The stock market defines large-cap as stocks that have a total market capitalization above $10 billion (around). Large-cap stocks tend to be more solid investments with low risk but fairly average returns. They also tend to have a longer history of proven success and a higher level of stability than smaller companies, which means that it's easier for them to maintain their position in the market.

- **Mid-Caps**: Mid-caps are companies with a total market capitalization that's somewhere between small and large-caps. They're relatively stable in terms of growth potential, but they also carry more risk than small-caps (though less risk than large-caps). These companies are successful enough to keep up with the larger companies, but they also still have room to grow and develop.

As you can see, all three of these classifications come with their own set of pros and cons, including risk and opportunity. Small-caps are great if you're looking for a chance to take a big leap in your portfolio's growth because they tend to be the most volatile of the bunch. However, large-caps carry a bit less risk but also offer lower growth potential. Mid-caps are able to maintain stability while still allowing the possibility for very heavy returns, though neither of those is guaranteed. The third reason is that it helps you make sure that all of your investments fall into line with each other so that they're able to work together smoothly without clashing or becoming ineffective.

How Stocks Can Make Money: Dividends and Capital Appreciation

Dividends are distributions of a company's profits to its shareholders. When you invest in stocks, you're buying shares in publicly traded companies. When the company pays dividends, it decides how much money it wants to distribute—usually, an investor would want as much as possible. Basically, any dividends are one of the ways that stockholders can receive some return on their investment.

Capital appreciation is when the value of your stocks goes up over time—and when this happens, so does your investment! If you buy a stock for $10 and sell it for $15 soon after that (and without touching the money), then you've made a capital profit or gain of 50%. It's like buying a car and re-selling it for more money than you paid—it's your profit.

Together, these two forms of returns, are what investors hope for when they invest in stocks. When you buy stock in a company, you expect to be able to sell later at a higher price (and if it doesn't go up in value—then you're stuck with it).

Dividends can be paid out quarterly or once a year. Capital appreciation is not necessarily predictable—but time plays the biggest factor in increasing price of stocks. As time passes, companies earn more profits from their investments and profits from previous quarters (which increases the amount of money that they can pay to shareholders).

Stock Vs. Bond

Stocks and bonds are two of the most common investments in the finance world. Investors might be surprised to find that there is a lot of overlap, but major differences, between stocks and bonds. Unlike stocks, bonds are not traded on public exchanges. Rather, they are pieces of paper with a set value and years to maturity assigned by the issuer. Bonds are issued for wide array of purposes (government funding, corporate investment) with many covenants that allow them to be traded on secondary exchanges after an initial issuance date (buying on the secondary market). Bonds also have a much higher interest rate than stocks. A bond is basically an IOU. If you purchase a bond from a government such as the U.S., you are essentially loaning money to the government with the expectation that you will be paid your principal plus interest at some point in the future when the bond matures.

A stock is also an IOU, but in this case it is issued by a private company rather than a government. When you buy stock in Apple (for example), you are essentially lending money to Apple for them to use as they see fit. The expectation is, of course, that Apple will use your money to grow profits and therefore pay you a dividend.

What is the difference?

Stocks are traded on public exchanges such as the New York Stock Exchange (NYSE) or NASDAQ while bonds are traded on secondary markets. There are many exchanges for bonds including the New York Stock Exchange and even bond-specific exchanges. These exchanges can trade globally around-the-clock as opposed to stocks which operate during pre-set hours each day.

Stocks generally have a much higher annual interest rate than bonds which can be as high as dozens of percentage points more than government-issued bonds.

Stocks can be bought and sold on secondary markets with greater ease than bonds which are generally only good for one trade. Bonds are sold at par value and then traded after so you are buying or selling a piece of paper (or electronic representation thereof) with an underlying value and par value.

How Stocks Are Traded

Stock trading is a way for investors to get a percentage of the profits generated by publicly-traded companies. Investors can purchase stocks either from an individual or from a broker.

Investors seeking to invest in stocks are usually hoping for an increase in the stock's price. When large numbers of shares are purchased, keeping prices high and increasing demand, this will lead to increased profits for the corporation that produces these stocks as well as larger dividends for investors. This is why investors often hope that they can win big when buying and selling shares on the stock market. Of course, because volatility is always a concern, there's no guarantee that investment will pay off and portfolios can quickly be depleted if risks aren't properly understood and managed appropriately. To purchase a stock, an investor has to have money available to pay for these stocks. They must then have a brokerage account with which to purchase the stocks. There are two kinds of brokerages; those that buy and sell stocks directly to investors, and those that trade for investors. The former is called a "full service" brokerage and the latter is called "discount."

Before an individual can cause stocks to be purchased on their behalf, they need to open a brokerage account with one of the many online brokers that are available today. These firms allow investors to conduct basic stock trading from their home computer by using Internet-based trading platforms, which offer tools like real-time market data, news feeds and online research capabilities. Investors who are interested in trading stocks can open a brokerage account with the broker of their choice and then deposit money into their new trading account. They will give the broker instructions as to how many shares they would like to purchase as well as where they want their shares of stock deposited.

Depending on the broker they choose, investors may be able to buy direct stocks and trade them online, have trades executed automatically by the brokerage firm at preset intervals or have trades executed more frequently. Most brokers allow investors to buy or sell stocks up until 4:00 p.m., after which time trades are only allowed if there is an "after-hours" market for the stock in question.

After opening an account and depositing money, investors can start trading stocks. Buy orders are placed with the broker and then filled by the company that issues the stock. Once this occurs, account values will reflect current prices for the stocks. Stock orders can be confirmed online or by phone and trades may be executed immediately or at times later in the day when after-hours markets open. After a trade is completed, investors will be able to access their online brokerage accounts to check their holdings' current value.

To sell stock, investors must sell their shares through the same brokerage firm they use to buy stocks. This can be done online or by phone, generally until 4:00 p.m. the same day. After that time, any trades not completed will carry over to the next trading day. Sell orders are placed and then executed at current market prices depending on the time of day the order goes through.

Some Definitions and Key Concepts Learned So Far

Stocks are one of the most popular forms of investments, representing shares in a company.

Certain stocks are more volatile than others, and it is possible for the stock to go up or down for various reasons.

A stock can also be an investment in a real estate property; here, a share is typically referred to as an interest. It can also refer to shares issued by credit unions.

The stock market is where you go to purchase stocks and bonds; it is also known as the equities market.

Stocks are quite intangible, but it's possible for them to be delivered in physical form; collecting stamps can be made into a hobby, and there is a stamp collecting stock exchange.

Some stocks are traded through the phone or internet, like household stocks at home.

When you own a share in a company, you are entitled to receive dividends from profits that the company claims.

The price of the stock fluctuates throughout time, so when you buy them at a certain point in time, you might earn more money if they increase in price over time. If you sell a stock before it expires, you have to pay tax on your earnings, but if you hold them for more than six months after the purchase date, the tax is usually lower. Companies pay out dividends when they generate profits; this money is then distributed among the shareholders. When a company keeps on failing to make enough money or if it doesn't generate any at all, stocks usually lose value and people who have invested in those stocks will suffer losses.

If you buy a share at 10 dollars and sell it two days later for 20 dollars, your profit would be 10 dollars minus commission costs.

If you have a 200 dollars stock portfolio, you can diversify by buying stocks from several companies. Companies are established to create profits and the shareholders are therefore entitled to receive part of those profits; this is the reason why dividends exist.

If you own stocks in a company, you are entitled to vote for it on certain matters concerning company policy and shares. Shareholders elect the board of directors, which is responsible for running different administrative duties at the company; they also approve different financial matters and even have an advisory role in many areas.

CHAPTER 6. EVALUATING STOCKS

Learn to Evaluate Companies and Their Numbers

A stockholder is a member of the public investing in a corporation for profit. They have a direct interest in the success of the company and its activities. It is therefore essential to use proper guidelines when assessing the value of an individual company. The following information will help you when evaluating companies for potential investment. The income statement provides an indication of how well a business is being run. It gives essential information about sales, costs, profits and assets used in the business at various times over a period of time. The balance sheet shows the financial strength and stability of a company at one point in time such as year-end, rather than with respect to time periods as with income statements. The statement of cash flows gives a picture of the operating cash flow of an organization. It is like a statement of income with an analysis provided for changes in working capital, investments, debt and equity. The gross margin ratio, used for comparing companies in the same industry, shows gross profit as a percentage of sales.

The first thing to determine is the fair value of the company. You can gain a lot of information from the annual report, particularly the notes to accounts (if applicable) and also from an investor relations website. It is not a one-step process; you have to take into account various factors. Generally there are two methods which can be used:

A discounted cash flow analysis (DCF), which models future cash flows, including growth and capital expenditure requirements against an assumed cost of capital. The discounted future cashflows are then added together to arrive at a value for the business. A DCF model can be used to modify the assumptions to gauge how changes in those assumptions could impact valuation. The variables in a DCF model include:

A simple price-to-earnings ratio (P/E), which is one of the most popular methods for valuing a company. It is arrived at by taking the company's earnings per share and dividing it by its current stock price. This method has its limits; there are many factors that influence earnings, which in turn impacts the P/E ratio. An example of this would be an extra expense caused by an unforeseen event, such as litigation costs or a major competitor going under. Good companies tend to have lower P/Es but the downside is that once the sector matures, competition will mean the price-to-earnings ratio will drop.

Does it have good profit margins?

The higher the better as long as expenses are not out of control and do not account for too high a percentage of total revenue when compared with other companies in the same sector or industry. The ideal profit margin would be in the upper quartile of its sector or industry peers. To find this out, you can consult a company's annual report or from an investor relations website.

Does the company have a good return on equity (ROE) and/or return on assets (ROA)? These would also be revealed in the annual reports and reported by an investor relations website. ROE should be equal to or more than that of its peers. ROA should be at least higher than its peers. It is worth noting that these two measures are used as benchmarks by analysts but are not perfect because factors other than efficiency influence them.

Is it earning money?

Gross profit percentage should be high and should be equal to or more than its peers. It is a good measure of how much after-tax profit a company is generating from sales. Gross profit is calculated by removing cost of goods sold from revenue and adding back depreciation and amortization expenses. The percentage can be compared with peers in its sector or industry by going through annual reports or checking an investor relations website. If it has a cash burn or, worse still, is losing money, that's not good.

The company should be able to earn at least enough money to pay for its ongoing operations and capital expenditure requirements as well as paying the interest on its loans. It is best if it has some cash left over which could be paid out as dividends or used in other ways such as buying back shares or investing in more profitable activities. If there is a significant difference in the amount of money it earns and the money it uses up, then that either means that there is too much capital expenditure required to maintain its current business activities or it is spending too much on interest payments on loans and other financial instruments.

Essential Stock Measurement

Whether you are a beginner or an experienced trader, there is always room to learn more about the top three stock measurements: market capitalization, outstanding shares, and EPS.

Market capitalization is calculated by multiplying the company's outstanding shares by its share price. Shares outstanding are how many of each company's stocks have been issued to shareholders. And finally, EPS shows the annual earnings per share of a company for the last quarter or year. These stock measurements are used by the financial markets and give you an idea of how a business performs financially. Market capitalization, outstanding shares, and EPS can be used to determine whether or not a company is undervalued or overvalued. You can use these stock measurements for your trading portfolio and research more information about companies that you are interested in trading with. *Market Capitalization*: Market capitalization gives investors a quick idea of the company's size versus other companies in its industry. If there are two companies with similar fundamentals, market capitalization may help you decide which one to buy. The market capitalization of a company is most often used to compare companies or industries.

Shares Outstanding: Shares outstanding are how many shares our company has issued to shareholders. This data can help us decide whether the company is overvalued or undervalued. Suppose we purchase a stock that has a high amount of shares outstanding. In that case, it's usually not because of the earnings per share but rather because the company thinks that there is still some room to grow and issue more shares after they've been floated to shareholders. As an investor, you should keep an eye on our position in companies with an excessive number of outstanding shares when determining whether or not the stock price is overvalued.

EPS: Earning per share is the amount of money the company has made in the past year. If a company made $3 million last year, then had an EPS of $2 per share, you would calculate that the annual earnings per share were $2 million. EPS data can also help determine whether a stock is overvalued or undervalued. If a stock has high EPS and, therefore, good earnings growth, we may think it should be more expensive than it is. On the other hand, if a stock has low EPS and loses money, we may think it's undervalued.

Stock's Split

Stock splits are one way that companies try to make their shares more attractive to investors. When this happens, every shareholder sees the number of shares they own double—but the price stays exactly the same. And while shareholders might seem like they've lost something by not owning twice as much as before, in reality, they now have ownership in twice as many companies.

CHAPTER 7. BUYING AND SELLING STOCKS

Stocks are pieces of ownership in a publicly-traded company. This is a method of raising money when starting a business, without actually giving up control over your company. It's also used for two situations: 1) businesses that have been in existence for several years that need extra cash to expand their operations, and 2) investors who need an investment vehicle for the long-term. The investors have purchased the stock with the expectation that its value will rise when a public corporation decides to sell shares to the public. You can also buy stocks on margin, which means you loan money from your broker to buy more stocks than you can afford to pay for in full at once. Stock trading—also called buying and selling stocks—is the process of buying one or more shares in a publicly-traded company. This gives you a financial stake in the company and entitles your name to either an equity or debt interest. Let's take a look at what it takes to buy stocks today.

How to Buy Stocks?

In order for a company to raise money and/or sell stock, they must publish or obtain a document that details:

a) The type of business the corporation is engaged in.

b) The specific shares available (the class or series).

c) The number of shares being issued, the par value per share, and whether there is a minimum subscription amount.

d) How sales will be handled (e.g., over-the-counter markets, U.S. Securities and Exchange Commission markets), who is authorized to sell the stock, etc...

e) Risk factors of the offer.

f) The company's financial statements.

g) Fees associated with the sale of the stock, such as those for registration services and brokers' commissions, if any.

h) Other important information such as an investment prospectus, pro forma statement, and other supplementary material.

Buying stocks can be a great way to secure your financial future... it can also be incredibly dangerous. So before you jump into stock trading without fully understanding the organization you are buying shares in, it is vital that you know what to look for in a company before buying its stock.

5 Tips for Buying Stocks

1. Have a Plan
2. Research Your Candidates
3. Look Before You Leap
4. Be Prepared to Lose Money
5. Be Ready to Act

How to Sell Stocks?

Selling stocks is the opposite of buying stocks. You are selling your shares to someone else. Just like with buying stocks, there are also many ways to sell them. You could sell them over-the-counter, through a stock exchange, or even over the internet.

Stocks are issued by corporations for raising money and/or publicly trading shares. They can be easily bought and sold just like any other financial security in exchange for legal tender (money). Stocks can represent either equity (ownership) interests in a firm or debt obligations of a firm, known as bonds. The stock market is the main financial market where stocks are traded. The New York Stock Exchange (NYSE), NASDAQ and other large exchanges are institutions designed to buy and sell stocks. There are many smaller stock markets around the world like the London Stock Exchange (LSE) and Japan Securities Dealers Automated Quotations (JPX).

Corporations issue stock in a process known as initial public offering or IPO. In this process, free shares are offered to the public through brokers, who will charge a commission for their services. The issuing company will use the money raised from selling these shares to fund operations or expand its business activities.

Buying and Selling Strategies: *growth* investing and *value* investing and their combination.

Growth Investing

Growth investing is all about choosing stocks that have a lot of potential and buying them while they're still undervalued. Let's illustrate that with an example. Suppose you buy a company with a price-earnings ratio (or PE) of 20 times in 2007, but the market suddenly crashes in 2008. In 2009, the PE ratio will soar to 30 times. At this point, it's time to sell if you want to make big money. On the other hand, suppose you bought a company with a PE ratio of 20 times in 2007, but in 2008 the market crashed, and its PE ratio became 10 times. In this case, you really didn't need to sell it because its PE ratio was still high. It's just that the stock price went down due to market conditions.

So, growth investing is all about buying shares of a company when its stock price is at an all-time low, and then selling shares when the share price is at an all-time high.

Value Investing

What is value investing? In essence, the basic principle behind value investing asserts that a company's stock price doesn't equate to its true worth. If this principle is correct then a company with seemingly mediocre prospects might still be undervalued and thus worth more than its current share price. Value investors seek out such opportunities to profitably purchase stocks at an advantageous price, then turn them around for a profit when the market realizes they are undervalued and prices them higher. Value investing can be broken down into two types of investment strategies, growth and value. Growth investors focus on buying stocks whose stock prices are expected to rise more than the market in general over the long-term due to the company's strong prospects, potential for rapid earnings growth and higher future dividend payments. Value investors focus instead on buying stock at a discount to its real (and sometimes hidden) earnings power (its true intrinsic value).

Combination of Growth and Value Investing

The stock market is the ultimate game of chance but there are ways for savvy investors to stack the odds in their favor. One way is by combining stocks that show promising growth with those generating returns through sound financial management. This strategy has been proven time and again as an effective way for investors to increase their capital while minimizing risk.

Companies that show potential for growth are exciting to watch. They expand into new markets and introduce new products, often expanding their revenue base at a rapid rate. Growth companies typically enjoy higher share prices because investors are enticed by the promise of future earnings. This is why investing in growth stocks is so powerful; if a company increases sales by 20 % a year it could see its revenue rise by more than half each year! This isn't to say that all growth companies will perform well in the long-term; there's always the possibility that they'll be unable to keep up with the pace of their competitors, or simply fail to adapt to changing circumstances. The biggest risk with growth stocks is that potential earnings growth (and revenue) will slow to a crawl or even reverse direction. For this reason, it's important to pair growth stocks with value stocks. Value companies are companies that have generated strong financial results while working within the constraints of their market environment and economic climate. They are able to grow, but in a controlled manner. Before investing, it's important to learn more about how each company's management team handles the tricky task of managing shareholder wealth effectively while still providing investors with a healthy return on investment.

Both growth and value stocks are valued based on their dividend income and earnings per share, but the way a company is valued is determined by the price-to-earnings ratio (P/E). Valuation is measured by dividing the stock's price by its earnings. Companies that are trading below their P/E ratio are considered undervalued; these companies typically see higher returns in the long-term.

Buying on a Margin

Margin buying is the process of borrowing capital from a broker in order to buy equity securities. This form of trading is only available for those who can afford it, unless the company has an arrangement with their brokerage firm that permits employees or directors who are not "technically" qualified to trade stocks on margin.

Margin buying will often result in both gains and losses on the account where borrowed funds are being used; this may take a toll on your pocketbook if you do not have sufficient cash reserves in comparison with your stock holdings.

The investor borrows the money and pays interest on it to the broker. The investor buys stocks with the borrowed cash. The portfolio is then monitored daily, and an investor will know whether to buy more shares based on what happens in the marketplace.

For example, if you have $10,000 in your account and you want to buy 1,000 shares of XYZ at $5, then you will be buying on margin. Your broker may allow you to borrow an additional $8,000 so that your total purchase price is only $13,000 (or 20% of your investment). This is called buying "on a margin." If XYZ stock moves higher, you will not have to buy more shares of XYZ or pay for the shares that you already own. They would be considered "free" because your initial cash investment is less than the total amount invested in the stock.

The greater the percentage that you invest, and the better your broker determines to be able to lend money, the larger your purchase price can be. You can use margin purchasing for most of your portfolio or just a portion of it.

When buying on margin, it is important to know that you are committing yourself to maintain minimum equity (i.e. maintenance margin) in your account at all times. If the equity in your account falls below this minimum, then an automatic "margin call" will be made. A margin call requires you to add more money to the account or sell enough stock to bring the equity up above the maintenance margin requirement within a set period of time. You will need to contact your broker before the margin call is initiated.

Trade What You Know

How many times have you heard the saying, "*It's better to trade what you know*," only to find that it's not necessarily true? If you're trading silver stocks and the market is going in a bearish direction, what good is it to trade what you know when that knowledge is going to create losses? Before you close your account and say that trading isn't for you, consider that many successful traders trade what they know. It's not enough to trade what they do or think. They must also have an understanding of why they are making the trades. For example, let's say you're bullish on a certain stock.

There are three reasons why you shouldn't make the trade:

1. You don't know what the catalyst is for the price move.

2. The new information doesn't change anything about your analysis of this company or its stock price.

3. You don't know why other people are trading this company or its related products right now.

If you haven't done any research on this company and you don't have an understanding of its products or related businesses, stay away from the trade. You can't say with any certainty that you know why people are willing to buy the stock right now. If you don't know why people are trading it, it's not a good idea for you to trade it.

Trading what you know could also mean trading what you do, as in the case of a commodities trader who has experience doing business in Africa. One year ago, he made a huge profit on coffee futures at this time of the year.

His question is: What should he do this year? Should he trade the same way that he did last year, or should he trade it differently because he thinks everyone else will be trading the same way that they did last year?

What does "trading what you know" mean in this case? How do you determine if you should trade the coffee futures in the same manner as last year? Or why would you change your trading approach from last year? You could use a technical approach with a moving average and trend line. Some traders will set up the strategy in advance before they enter into trades. Others may use an algorithmic approach, letting their software program run and set stops and targets.

Either way, before you begin to trade, you should ask yourself the following questions:

1. What is my goal for trading coffee futures this year? Am I trading to make money or am I trading to learn more about the market?

2. How much money do I want to risk on this trade?

3. How many contracts of coffee futures do I want to buy?

4. What is my risk/reward ratio for this trade and how much am I willing to lose on the trade?

5. Have I picked a support or resistance level that will tell me when to get out of the trade?

6. What is my exit-strategy if the market tries to pull back before it touches the support or resistance level? Do I ride it out or get out immediately?

7. Do I have a stop-loss order in place so that I can get out of the trade if something unexpected happens?

8. Am I trading only one contract, two contracts, or some number of contracts depending on how much money I want to risk on this trade?

9. Have I decided how much profit I want to make on this trade?

10. Do I have a time-frame for the trade?

11. What is my risk-reward ratio for this trade if the market goes against me?

12. What is Plan B if Plan A doesn't work out as planned?

Using these questions as a guideline, you can determine if you should simply trade what you know or if you should change your strategy in some way.

When many people think of the term "trade," they might think of a market where goods or services are bought and sold. But trading, in its most general sense, is the act of exchanging one thing for another. And there's no better time to trade than when you're a teenager—when you have fewer responsibilities and more time to explore your interests.

The following list includes some examples of companies that teens can swap their knowledge for some great perks: Apple, Disney, Tesla, Netflix, Amazon, Nike and Adidas. Sony also has indies games like Journey available that require an age range from 13–18 in order to play it.

While some of these are specific examples, the general idea is that companies think of their younger audience when they design and program their products. Some businesses even go so far as to release mobile apps specifically for teens. As a result, companies find themselves in a unique position to engage with a younger audience. With this in mind, teens often take advantage of these opportunities. With the right computer skills and a willingness to learn, they can contribute something valuable to the business themselves—even if they're just helping out on a project or answering the phones for the part-time hours required in their job description. For example, one high school senior built Apple's Siri-inspired virtual assistant software into his mobile phone app. Of course, this list is far from exhaustive. It's also worth mentioning that not all of these companies are easy to get into. Apple and Tesla, for example, offer internships that require an interview and a college degree—but the internship at Apple may be tough for those who are currently in high school. Netflix requires teens to be 18 years old to join their streaming service; for Disney it's at least 12 years old; Nike and Adidas have age restrictions as well; while Sony games tend to be rated only for those 13 and up.

And of course, most of these jobs can lead to career opportunities, where kids can grow with the company, they have been trading their knowledge with. Some teens even find themselves working in the industry they have been a fan of for years.

Apple

There's a reason why so many teens have an iPhone: Apple designs everything with its younger audience in mind. Take the iPod Touch, for example, which is built with games and apps that appeal to younger users. Today, Apple has over 500 employees dedicated to developing products and services that appeal specifically to teens. That translates into innovative products like the earbuds that come included with the iPhone 7—something that might seem silly, but could be very useful to teens who are always on the go.In addition, Apple has an internship program called the "Undergraduate Program" that has as many as 20,000 applications submitted each year. Although it's geared for college students, high schoolers can still apply and have a shot at landing a spot in the program. According to Apple's website, "The Undergraduate Program" is a broad-based training and development program designed to teach college students about Apple and its products. The company hires 10 students from around the world each year. This sounds like a dream job for any teen willing to get involved in the tech industry—especially since applicants will undoubtedly be able to put that experience on their resume once they get out of college.

Disney

Although Disney is known for its family-friendly content, the company has always had a knack for marketing to younger audiences. It also has an internship program with opportunities for teens who have an interest in the entertainment industry. Disney offers a diverse set of internship positions, which can span from animal care to engineering and everything in between. As part of the internship, interns at Disney can expect to have interaction with senior leaders and get a behind-the-scenes look at how their favorite films are put together. However, there are a few requirements that must be met in order to apply: Interns must be at least 17 years old and maintain full-time status during their internship. Interns are also required to attend seminars, offer insight on improving the parks and resorts, and be able to work a flexible schedule.

Tesla

Thanks to companies like Tesla, it's now possible for teens to look at cars as something that can be stylish and fun. Many of Tesla's vehicles have a dashboard touchscreen in the middle of the car. Not only does it control all of the vehicle settings, but it's also integrated with Apple CarPlay—which is another way that teens can interact and use their phones while driving. In addition to all of this, Tesla also has an internship program geared toward students who are pursuing careers in engineering or business. According to Tesla's website, internships can last up to 10 weeks, and may include dynamic work environments in one of the company's factories, retail stores or service centers. The most important thing to remember about these internships is that they follow all laws and safety standards. No intern will ever be put in a dangerous position during an internship with Tesla.

Netflix

To be a Netflix member, you have to be at least 18 years old, but there are plenty of opportunities for teens looking to get into the entertainment industry. For example, Netflix offers paid summer internship programs that prepare high school students for future careers in content acquisition and production for the streaming video service. These programs offer participants an opportunity to study how Netflix selects shows for its library and go through an immersive process of learning how to write and produce their own shows.

Overall, the goal of these programs is to have the best possible candidates that can take over the company someday. Considering the positions are paid, these internships are ideal for teens who have aspirations of working in Hollywood.

Amazon

Amzon has a variety of internship opportunities, including many that are geared toward teens. Amazon Warehouse is an internship program that gives participants the chance to learn how to work in a warehouse and how Amazon's supply chain works. Another option is the Customer Service Representative Internship, which gives interns the opportunity to get their foot in the door by getting hired as a full-time customer services representative after completing their internship with Amazon.

This position involves working with customers and training new hires on how to take care of customers' questions and concerns. If you think your teen has what it takes, they might want to consider applying for one of these internships.

CHAPTER 8. INDEX AND MUTUAL FUNDS

An index fund is a mutual fund that attempts to replicate the performance of some broader securities market index. Index funds are passively managed (i.e., they track their target index rather than selecting individual stocks). Index funds typically charge low fees because they do not require high-paid managers and because they don't trade often.

Mutual funds are investment companies that pool monetary contributions from many people, which enables investments in stocks, bonds and other securities. Today most mutual funds are indexed for tracking the performance of stocks or bonds according to a preselected group of securities, known as an index. Such indices usually include common stocks traded on U.S. and Canadian exchanges.

An index fund is not the same thing as an index. An index is composed of a set of securities, such as the S&P 500, that represent a segment of the market or economy. An index cannot be purchased; rather it exists to serve as a benchmark for investors who want to track how their portfolios are performing against the market or have some other basis for comparison.

A mutual fund that tracks its benchmark closely is said to be "indexed." Other funds in the same family invest in individual stocks and bonds, and these are not indexed. Indexing has proven itself to be more efficient than active management: The average annual return of actively managed U.S.

To buy and sell index funds or mutual funds it necessitates that you have a record with a broker, for example, TD Ameritrade, TD Trade King, E*Trade, Scottrade and so on. Mutual fund investing is best for amateurs who would prefer not to stress over monetary occasions that influence stocks and may lose cash in the event that they got passionate during conditions such as these. Buying into mutual funds are extraordinary for some investors to get going with since, supposing that they don't have the opportunity to do the examination and buy stocks at that point investing in mutual funds can broaden their arrangement of stocks and help them feel greater. When buying an index fund or a mutual fund there are three unique sorts to look over. The main kind is called an "open-finished" fund which implies that anybody can buy and sell whenever during the day anyway the individuals who buy or sell on the open market won't get as positive of a cost as the individuals who invest straightforwardly from the organization's site. The subsequent sort is known as a "shut finished" fund which implies that they just offer a restricted measure of offers. When these offers have sold, which can require days or even weeks, the fund will presently don't permit anybody to buy into it. The third and most ideal approach to buy an index fund or mutual fund is known as a "no-heap" fund. A no-heap fund is actually what it says, you won't ever pay any charges to invest in this particular mutual fund. The individuals who invest in a no-heap index fund or mutual fund will get the very value that the organization gets for selling shares.

Something vital to acknowledge is that it takes cash to bring in cash. It doesn't bode well to buy an index fund and clutch it for a very long time on the off chance that you won't reinvest any of the increases from your underlying investment into more portions of a similar mutual fund. Thusly, it is a smart thought to invest sufficient cash in an index fund or mutual fund so you can buy extra offers each time you have abundance capital since nobody can anticipate what the stock market will do throughout an extensive stretch of time.

There are various sorts of index funds and mutual funds to invest in. The main sort is called an "Index Fund" which tracks an index, for example, the S&P 500, Dow Jones 30 Industrial Average or the NASDAQ Composite. These funds will hold each and every stock that is in the index which implies that it expands your possessions by spreading your cash across thousands of stocks. This is quite possibly the main elements of a mutual fund on the grounds that since one stock performed ineffectively throughout some undefined time-frame doesn't imply that all other stocks in the index fund will do inadequately also. Along these lines, since you are expanding your possessions by buying thousands of various stocks with only a few hundred dollars you will encounter less instability in your portfolio.

The second sort of mutual fund is known as a "Profit Income Fund." These funds will invest in profit-paying stocks, for example, those which deliver profits to furnish their investors with pay. Normally these funds will have a huge segment of their property in service organizations, land organizations and even some medical care stocks.

The third sort of mutual fund is called a "Functioning Management Fund" which implies that the manager of the fund can make various kinds of investments other than buying the entirety of the stocks in the index. The dynamic management fund can likewise buy securities, unfamiliar monetary forms or even wares inside your portfolio.

The last sort of mutual fund is known as a "Fund of Funds" which implies that it contains various kinds of mutual funds. When investing in a fund of funds you should search for one that has a few distinct sorts of funds so your cash is ensured against horrible showing in one explicit fund or index.

Whenever you have chosen to invest in an index fund or mutual fund then the most straightforward approach to buy offers would be through the organization straightforwardly since they will charge you less expenses. Nonetheless, in the event that you need more cash to make an immediate investment, at that point there is another approach to invest. You can generally begin with a limited quantity of cash and then reinvest the increases from your underlying investment in a similar mutual fund. On the off chance that you are simply beginning in the stock market it is significant that you don't buy an index fund or mutual fund without understanding what it does. Each mutual fund will normally have an outline which clarifies everything about that particular index fund or mutual fund. In the event that there are any inquiries concerning the fund, at that point you ought to circle back to a call to the organization.

CHAPTER 9. EXCHANGE TRADED FUNDS (ETFS)

ETFs (Exchange Traded Funds) are managed monetary instruments and not OTC (like forex) as they are traded on a controlled market, for example, the Italian stock exchange. For what reason do you need to understand what ETFs are and how they work, particularly in the event that you are new to monetary investments? I accept that ETFs are indeed "another" investment opportunity that until only a couple of years prior were shut to singular investors. ETFs permit the investor to accomplish more prominent self-rule and freedom from the financial framework; more noteworthy mindfulness in the decision of their investments. ETFs are a straightforward monetary instrument, both in their activity and use: therefore they can be utilized by any private investor who needs to invest their reserve funds autonomously. Consider an ETF a fund dressed as an activity ... in what sense? I'll clarify immediately. An ETF resembles a fund since it reproduces the arrangement of portions of a fund much the same as a mutual fund (the ETF, notwithstanding, is latently managed while the fund is effectively managed). Both the fund and the ETF permit you to differentiate on the market with a single tick since you don't need to physically choose the protections, however with a single tick you buy the instrument and you have a generally broadened investment. In any case, I envision that there are significant contrasts between mutual funds and ETFs, incorporating fundamentally lower costs in ETFs. You can investigate the subject in the article "*Contrasts among ETFs and funds: discover the amount you can save each year.*"

You can consider the ETF as a stock simultaneously on the grounds that you buy and sell it promptly as though it were a stock, at the current market cost. Consequently, from a functional perspective, buying an ETF is totally indistinguishable from buying a stock, yet what changes is the thing that is inside an ETF, that is its huge organization. To give you a culinary model, the activity is the single kind of a tub of frozen yogurt, the ETF is the tub of frozen yogurt, which can contain numerous flavors inside.

ETFs are an inactively managed apparatus.

ETFs are organized with the point of reproducing the arrival of a reference index (called "benchmark") as precisely as could be expected and not contribution a better yield than the actual benchmark.

This goal is accomplished just by holding the very offers that are essential for the reference index.

Buying an ETF, for example, the SPDR S and P500 ETF (Isin code IE00B6YX5C33), is comparable to buying with a solitary snap a bushel indistinguishable from that of the American S&P 500 index, which is comprised of 500 US organizations with the biggest capitalization.

So the presentation of your ETF follows that of the recreated index, accurately the Americans and P500 index.

Mutual funds, then again, are effectively managed monetary instruments, that is, there is a genuine manager who pays since it should cause you to get a better yield than the reference index. Sadly in 90% of cases (to be expansive and idealistic) this doesn't occur, yet you keep on paying significant expenses each year ... so I encourage you to begin asking yourself inquiries in the event that you have cash invested in funds.

5 Kinds of Exchange Traded Funds

1 - Index ETFs

Index ETFs inactively track a basic index. For instance, the Standard and Poor's 500 Index, which is contained the biggest organizations in the US market by market capitalization recorded on the NYSE or NASDAQ. At the point when you invest in an index ETF, you're investing in a container of protections addressing that specific index. Subsequently, in the event that your investment goes up, at that point this is on the grounds that your fundamental bushel did well too whether it depends on investable indexes, for example, security indexes or non-investable indexes, for example, product indexes.

2- ETFs that expect to follow a particular index and beat it

These ETFs hold the hidden protections in a similar extent as they show up in the index, however they are intended to outflank it. This implies that if, for instance, you're expecting a huge capital addition in a specific sector at that point you'd need to buy an ETF that intends to follow the benchmark yet with less unpredictability. For instance, you may invest in an ETF that tracks the S&P 500 Index yet invests 75% of its property in stocks with better-than-expected fundamentals, for example, high-income development and low obligation.

3 - Sector funds – US-based indexes

These mean to follow a particular sector, for example, innovation or medical services. In the event that you're hoping to invest in a particular sector, at that point you should consider an ETF that wagers on one of these sectors.

4 - Broadly diversified ETFs

These are like index ETFs and hold a crate of resources and track the index however have a more extensive range of possessions. While this implies more expansion it likewise implies less individual stock exploration is required. An investor who would not like to invest a lot of energy checking his investments may lean toward this kind of fund.

5 - Managed ETFs

These are effectively managed ETFs. They require crafted by an investment manager to supervise their property and are not attached to a specific index.

When would it be advisable for one to buy or sell an ETF?

The overall agreement is that if an individual investor might want to invest in the stock market yet doesn't have any desire to really buy and sell stocks by and large, at that point an ETF item might be the correct investment vehicle. In like manner, in the event that somebody needs openness to wares—yet don't have any desire to really buy and sell actual gold, silver or soybeans—at that point an item ETF will give this kind of openness. In the event that you are buying a specific ETF as long as possible and intend to keep it there until you need your cash then you can hang on until retirement. Then again, in the event that you intend to trade all the more effectively and have the opportunity to do as such, at that point there might be times when you should buy and sell ETFs.

For instance, if stock markets enter a drawn-out down cycle, an investor may choose to get out there and buy stocks at these lower levels after a rectification to supplant those stocks that are currently failing to meet expectations of their benchmarks. At such a period, selling their ETF offers and buying singular stocks would give this kind of openness. There was one specific person who purchased shares in a little cap esteem ETF against the exhortation of many Wall Street experts. He held his situation during the 2008 market decline and today is quite possibly the most over-utilized, yet additionally perhaps the most beneficial investors out there.

Alternately, if markets are going up for an all-inclusive timeframe as they have been as of late, an ETF investor may choose to get out there and sell their possessions to take benefits. Once more, selling their offers and buying singular stocks would give such openness. As of late we have seen numerous investors who sold their possessions of little cap esteem ETFs to buy huge cap esteem stocks (e.g., iShares Russell 2000 Value Index Fund versus iShares S&P 500 Value Index Fund). While this methodology is an incredible method to support one's wagered, it isn't prudent to roll out such radical improvements at the same time.

While there are a few dangers and intricacies related to investing in ETFs, people who set aside the effort to teach themselves the thing they are buying ought to have the option to maintain a strategic distance from a portion of the entanglements. What is significant is that investors in ETFs recollect that these investments are not resistant to extraordinary descending changes since they may have done above and beyond the long-haul.

CHAPTER 10. OTHER TYPES OF INVESTMENTS

Cryptocurrencies

The first ever cryptocurrency, Bitcoin was invented in 2009 by a person or group of people using the name Satoshi Nakamoto. The idea behind Bitcoin was to produce a currency independent of any central authority, transferable electronically, more or less instantly with very low transaction fees.

Since then many other cryptocurrencies have emerged as the value and use of cryptocurrencies has been growing exponentially. In late 2017 prices skyrocketed for bitcoin and other cryptocurrencies but have since stabilized again.

Cryptocurrencies use a technology called blockchain to record transactions. Blockchain is a decentralized and distributed public ledger that is used by cryptocurrencies. It is basically an electronic payment system, in which peer-to-peer users can make payments without using a central bank or single administrator, with the transactions recorded chronologically and publicly.

What number of cryptocurrencies are there? What are they worth?

In excess of 6,700 distinctive cryptocurrencies are exchanged freely, as indicated by CoinMarketCap.com, a market research site. Also, cryptocurrencies keep on multiplying, fund-raising through starting coin contributions, or ICOs. The complete value of all cryptocurrencies on Feb. 18, 2021, was more than $1.6 trillion, as indicated by CoinMarketCap, and the absolute value of all bitcoins, the most mainstream advanced money, was fixed at about $969.6billion.

Gold and Silver

In the modern-day and age, our world is one of financial crisis and global economic instability. People worry most about what may happen if an unthinkable event takes place. But regardless, many people are looking for a way to protect their hard-earned money from ever-changing economic trends.

Gold and silver investments are one of the best ways to protect your money from lost value in currency fluctuations due in countries with unstable economies. The problem is that many people still don't understand what these investments entail or how they work, which causes them to miss out on a great opportunity to save their hard-earned cash.

Private Equity

Private equity investments are a way to get rich quick. They are short-term, high-risk investments in which investors buy an ownership stake in a company, usually with the aim of reselling it for profit at a later date. Since they're not as regulated as traditional stock markets, private equity deals can offer investors higher returns than stocks and bonds on average. On the other hand, if the market turns against you then you can lose all of your money in private equity investing much faster than you would with stocks or bonds. So although private equity may be more lucrative on average, it's also riskier than other types of investments—and that's something to keep in mind before you invest.

Hedge Funds

Hedge funds are investment vehicles that aim to generate capital gains or income by taking advantage of market price fluctuations. There are many different types of hedge funds, limited only by the imagination and expertise of the fund's creators.

For example, a macro hedge fund may bet on currency movements in different countries, while a relative value hedge fund might look for discrepancies in debt instruments with similar risk profiles but different prices.

All types rely on sophisticated financial strategies and lucrative information to generate profits. Of course, this is not without risk; all investments come with some kind of chance for loss.

Ethical Investments

Ethical investment is the act of taking your money and investing it in entities that support your values. It's pretty straightforward, really. If you want to invest in a company who isn't going to treat their employees poorly, you can look for companies that have employees with benefits and good working conditions. You can look for companies who don't take advantage of people or resources they shouldn't be using.

The concept has been around since the early 1900s when the idea of separation between church and state came to exist in all that mattered—you couldn't get one without the other if we wanted society to progress as a whole. Nowadays, many people are very supportive of ethical investment and other related practices. For example, one of the ways you can invest ethically is to put your money in banks that support renewable resources and energy sources. If you're looking to invest ethically, the first thing you need to do is remove your money from any banks or institutions that have a bad reputation for exploiting their workers or customers.

#1 – Investments Based on Social Values

Cultural standards direct what is worthy of a specific culture and what isn't. These are normally implanted in various social orders and societies and are generally acknowledged inside that specific culture. Considering the cultural values and what could be gainful to society all in all, preceding making ventures is one type of moral contributing. For instance, a co-usable society is the best illustration of speculations dependent on cultural values. Individuals from a specific culture structure a co-employable and put resources into it. At the point when any individual from the general public requires reserves, the co-usable society progresses cash to that specific part. For this situation, the speculation is made by the individuals from the general public, considering the prosperity of the general public overall—including every one of its individuals.

#2 – Investments dependent on Moral Values

Regularly, this type of contributing would go under the "negative effect" class. A financial backer would not put resources into any industry/company that doesn't line up with his/her virtues. For instance, investors would not be inclined to putting resources into tobacco/alcohol fabricating organizations if the financial backer has solid emotions that such enterprises are against their ethics.

#3 – Investments dependent on Religious Values

Each religion has its own practices, convictions, and culture. What is adequate to one society may not be worthy to another. Individuals from a specific religion/culture would be more disposed to put resources into businesses/organizations that are valuable to their way of life/religion or assembling items that are adequate to their way of life/religion.

For instance, investors in the Middle East would be more disposed to put resources into Hijab/Abaya producing organizations as there is a gigantic interest for it, and it is worthy to that specific culture.

Financial backers having a place with the Judaism confidence would be more disposed to put resources into organizations that cling to their standards—like Kosher nourishments.

#4 – Investments dependent on Political Values

The political environment influences the manner in which the financial backers see the condition of the economy and normally impacts their contributing examples. Financial backers will in general contribute more and accept the danger to be lower when their ideological group is in force. Financial backers are bound to hold stocks and put resources into long-haul protections during such period. On the other hand, financial backers would be more averse to contribute when an alternate ideological group is in force. They would be bound to put resources into momentary stocks and exchange all the more frequently.

For instance, a leftist would probably put more in the stock market when the Democrat Party is in force and would put resources into ventures that favor the specific party's value framework.

#5 – Investments dependent on Environmental Values/Green Investing

Given the present status of the planet, green putting is quickly acquiring significance lately. Under this sort of contributing, speculations are made in organizations that produce harmless to the ecosystem items, or their assembling measures are economy amicable. There have been numerous examples in the course of recent many years wherein huge scope enterprises have caused significant air/water contaminations. These influence the condition of the climate significantly.

Green putting centers around putting resources into organizations which don't hurt the climate through their creation measures just as the eventual outcome is climate agreeable. It isn't adequate that the cycles are climate amicable if the eventual outcome ends up being something unsafe, for example, single-use plastics or choose renewable energy sources for your home.

Green contributing additionally centers around different organizations which have an ecological agreeable target, for example:

- Protection of existing characteristic assets;
- Finding and delivering elective fuel sources;

- Reusing;
- Tidying up of water bodies;
- Green transportation;
- Decreasing of wastage.

Coins, Stamps and Art

Coins

Some people might think investing in coins is too risky, but there are actually a lot of ways to ensure that you don't lose money. The first thing you need to do is find out what kind of coin you want to invest in. Should it be a smaller coin that has potential for big gains? A more established coin with a lower risk factor? Or something else entirely? Choosing the right investment can make or break your decision so make sure you take the time to understand the different options available for your portfolio. The second step would be determining where and how much money you want to invest. No matter how much you hold, it is still a good idea to spread your money across multiple different coins. Not only does this provide a safety net in case one investment goes wrong, but it can also help with the tax implications as well. Different states have varying laws regarding cryptocurrency so make sure you keep up with the latest news if you are going to be investing from an outside location.

The third step would be to actually make your move and invest in a coin. The ideal time to buy would be during big dips in the coin's prices such as when Bitcoin went from $30,000 to $6000 dollars or when Ethereum went from $1000 to $200 this year. The best thing about cryptocurrency is that there is virtually no way for the market to be controlled by a single party. This is one of the reasons why it has experienced such success in recent years. All it takes is one bad round of news or a regulatory decision to cause coins prices to drop, so if you're in it for the long-haul then now would be the time to buy.

Stamps

A true stamps investor knows both the past and present of this commodity, as well as how to find the best stamps for investment.

How valuable do you think it would be to have a physical commodity that has been used since ancient times for communication? It turns out that these postage stamps were first used in Great Britain in 1840 and the United States around 1850. Hence, postage stamps are not only an invaluable part of the history of communications but also a tangible investment.

Art

The art world has always been shrouded in mystery. It takes a deep knowledge or a refined eye to identify the value of an artwork. Yet, every day, people are buying art as an investment for their future retirement funds. According to the Claymore Group's "2017 Global Fine Art Market Report," more than half of total sales of top-tier art (works valued at $1 million or more) took place at auctions on record-breaking days for most impressive bids. In 2017, Asia was the biggest market for high-end art sales, with collectors from Hong Kong and mainland China leading the way. Furthermore, art has outperformed all other categories of collectible asset over the last 20 years.

The Top Ten Art markets are as follows:

1. China, $8 billion (grew by 20% in 2014)

2. United States, $5.2 billion (up 20% in 2014)

3. United Kingdom, $3.5 billion (up 20% in 2014)

4. France, $2.8 billion (up 15% in 2014)

5. Japan, $1.9 billion (down 1% in 2014)

6. Germany, $1.7 billion (down 3% in 2014)

7. India, $1 million or more per piece (growing 40%)

8. Switzerland, art valued at over $250 million for the first time ever during the period

9. South Korea: art valued at over $250 million for the first time ever during the period

10. Russia, art valued at over $250 million for the first time ever during the period

A sample of works which set record prices at auction:

1. "Nu Couché" by Amedeo Modigliani (1917), sold for $170.4 million on November 12, 2015 in New York City.

2. "White Center" (1952) by Mark Rothko sold for $66.8 million on May 8, 2016 in New York City to an unknown buyer but was later revealed to be Kenneth C. Griffin, founder and chief executive of Citadel Investment Group and CEO of Citadel LLC.

3. "The Card Players" (1891) by Paul Cézanne sold for $250 million on November 11, 2014 in New York City.

In late 2013, billionaire Ken Griffin bought an artwork by abstract artist Mark Rothko for $80.1 million and a Jackson Pollock painting (1948) for $200 million. Bloomberg News reported that he and his wife Anne Dias Griffin purchased the two artworks from David Geffen, co-founder of DreamWorks SKG. "*I collect art today not just because I can afford to do so, but also because I can afford not to do so,*" Griffin said in a press release at the time.

Comics Market (Rare Editions, First Editions, Special Editions)

X-Men No. 1 (Rare Edition)

In 2012, the introduction issue of X-Men from 1963 sold for $492,937 at sell-off. The close mint duplicate acquired a 9.8 out of 10 on the CGC scale, the measurement utilized by authorities to decide the nature of vintage funnies. The issue presented Cyclops, Beast, and Magneto (Wolverine wouldn't appear for one more decade).

Tales of Suspense No. 39 (Rare Edition)

Iron Man was viewed as a B-list Marvel superhuman for quite a long time—until 2008, when the film variation pushed the character into the spotlight. The buzz around Iron Man made his introduction issue from 1963, Tales of Suspense

No. 39, a standout amongst other selling funnies from the time when it sold for $375,000 in 2012.

"Stunning Fantasy #15," in which Spider-Man first shows up, slipped to second-most noteworthy Marvel comic at any point unloaded, having sold for $1.1 million of every 2011. (First Edition).

Assassin's Creed Origins TPB (2020 Titan Comics) Special Edition

Composed by Anne Toole and Anthony Del Col. Workmanship by PJ Kaiowa. Cover by Toni Infante. Back Cover by Sanya Anwar and Special Edition of direct connection to the top-rated videogame, *Assassin's Creed Origins* including at no other time seen restrictive substance.

Old Egypt, a place that is known for greatness and interest, is vanishing in a merciless battle for power. Disclose dim mysteries and failed to remember legends as we excursion to the actual beginnings of the Assassin Brotherhood and past!

Superman (1938 - Action Comics #1) Rare Edition

The issue of Action Comics #1, which sold for 10 cents when it was released in 1938, is the world's most valuable comic book. The comic includes the story of Superman's origins and is considered to be the start of the superhero genre, has sold for a record $3.25 million. It is thought only around 100 copies of the comic still exist.

This particular copy was "buried in a stack of old 1930s movie magazines", was in mint condition, and shows the first ever appearance of Superman.

CHAPTER 11. THE RIGHT TIME AND THE RIGHT WAY TO INVEST

There has never been a more important time to invest your money in stocks than right now. With the American economy looking good and inflation rates low, you should be taking advantage of this opportunity as soon as possible. Owning stocks can help you make a lot of money with little risk of failure, so let's go over everything you need to do before investing in them. It's a safe bet that you've heard of the stock market. Many people invest in stocks, bonds, commodities, and other options to try and build up their retirement funds. But when is the right time to invest?

The answer is different for everyone. Some people are comfortable investing in volatile markets while others prefer the stability of government bonds or gold bullion. Ultimately it comes down to your risk tolerance and what you hope to get out of your investment decisions. Uncertainty is never a good thing, but it does have the positive effect of creating opportunities for those who are willing to take a chance and invest. In fact, it's the most successful investors that take advantage of these situations. If you can't play the game, you can't win! You have to be flexible and ready to adjust your strategy to any unexpected events that might occur. Keep this in mind when deciding how much time you plan on investing in your stocks or bonds.

In certain situations, there are rules that apply to all investors. When deciding to invest in stocks, start looking at companies with steady earnings growth, low debt levels and a solid quarterly report. It's important to keep an eye on these things before investing in them.

You always want to know what your return rate is, which is based on the compounded annual growth of a stock. For example, if you invest in a stock and it has a return rate of 10% then at the end of one year, you'll have made 10%. Multiply that by 4 and you'll see that after 4 years your earnings will be 40%. You will have doubled your investment in only four years. This type of investment is known as long-term and should be considered by investors who are comfortable with risk. This is because there are no guarantees that the company will continue to have solid earnings and a positive report. If this happens, though, you'll be able to sell your stock and make a profit.

Then there's the option of short-term. This involves taking larger amounts of money in smaller investments because of the faster returns. Basically you are playing the market by buying stocks that show high volatility and fast growth rates, holding them for one year or less then selling them off. This is an option for investors who want to make a lot of money quickly but aren't willing to risk losing it all if they invest in the wrong stock.

The last option is known as fix dividend income investing. You invest in these types of stocks by getting dividends, which are basically a percentage of the company's earnings.

The return rate for this type of investment is rather small and is more suited to investors who want to keep their money safe. This isn't exactly the type of investment your retirement needs but it's good to have something like it as a safety net.

Setting Your SMART Financial Goals

Setting your SMART financial goals may seem daunting, especially if you have no idea where to start. Let's break it down into a few simple steps to make this process less overwhelming:

- Choose a goal as specific as possible for your savings and investments: For example, do you want to save $1,000 or $10,000? Choose the amount that is appropriate for your needs and budget.

- Establish specific dates for these goals by asking yourself what you need them by: Perhaps you need an emergency fund by next year. Or maybe you want to create a college fund for five years from now. Time frames will differ based on individual saving needs.

- Assign a specific amount of money to each goal: After you know how much you want to save for each goal, just break it down into monthly amounts.

- Set up a Smart financial goals system: Once you have established your goals, it's time to put a plan in place so that you can allocate funds appropriately. You can start by setting up an automatic withdrawal from your checking account or a recurring transfer from your savings account into your investment account.

5 Pitfalls to Avoid

1) **Avoid Scams** —This is the one tip that should be repeated 10 times over. As tempting as it may be to make quick money, be wary of any money you can make quickly. The easiest way to spot a scam is if there is an element of secrecy. If someone wants you to give them your credit card number in order to cash out your investment earnings or if they are trying to keep the investment a secret, just run the other way!

2) **Avoid Tax Evasion** —No matter how large the amount that you invest into a product, never buy into anything that does not have your capital gains in mind. Your interest is always in getting your money back with a reasonable profit, and this should always be on the top of your mind when investing.

3) **Avoid Cash Out** —When you invest, you are always hoping to make more than what you put in. Otherwise what's the point? However, when it comes to certain investments that do not have a set pay-out system, never cash out early. The only reason to cash out early would be if you need the money for some emergency, and even then, you should try and use other methods. For example, selling your home or getting a USAA auto loan.

Even those 40 % returns can quickly turn into 0 % when you cash out early

4) **Avoid ACH Payments** —This one is included in almost every list on avoiding risky investments. While this kind of sounds like a loophole to get away from paying taxes, the IRS has closed it with a cap on interest rates. If you are looking to avoid paying capital gains taxes, do not use an ACH payment system for your investment.

5) **Not knowing your own level of risk tolerance** — Investors often fail to know what their own risk tolerance is when investing in the market. People who invest in stocks should have a "stomach" for risk. They should be ready to endure short-term losses in order to achieve long-term gains. Knowing your risk tolerance also means that you know the amount of risk you can take. If you have a low tolerance for risk, take on smaller amounts of stocks and mutual funds if possible. You don't want to put yourself at the point where your money is never safe from losing value.

CHAPTER 12. HOW TO MANAGE YOUR INVESTMENT PORTFOLIO

You can't depend on karma. To win large in the stock market, you must have a strategy. You should utilize rationale and do broad examination. The following are the most impressive portfolio management techniques that you can use to develop your cash and make the best out of your investment portfolio.

Strategy 1.

Try Not to Use Your Emotions in Making Investment Decisions

Charlie is a prepared stock market investor and has brought in a great deal of cash in the past from his investments in the assembling business. Following years and years of winning in the stock market, he chose to invest in games stocks. He examined various games stocks including Madison Square Garden Co. (MSG).

MSG claims five pro athletics groups, including the New York Knicks.

Its stock worth is somewhat unpredictable and changes habitually, so it's not incredible for long-haul investment. However, Charlie is a New York Knicks fan, so he invested in MSG and in the long run lost a ton of his well-deserved cash.

You will lose a ton of investment openings in the event that you let your feelings cloud your judgment. You should be very target when you're choosing which stocks to invest in. You should save your own inclinations and take a gander at the numbers.

You can uphold your games group all you need, however don't buy a group's unsteady stock since you're a lifelong fan.

Strategy 2.
Diversification

The insightful men of Wall Street always say "don't tie up your resources in one place." Why? All things considered, in the event that you lose that crate, you'll wind up losing all your eggs. You should share your riches. For instance, on the off chance that you have an investment financial plan of $20,000 don't spend everything on FB stocks. Buy various stocks and different protections. You can invest shortly in stocks and a tad in bonds and testaments of store. One of the least expensive and most straightforward ways to expand your investment is to invest in a mutual fund. You can likewise invest in exchange-traded fund or ETFs and land investment trusts or REITs.

It's additionally savvy to invest a smidgen of your cash in index funds. The best index funds like S&P 500 permits you to claim a tad of the most elevated performing stocks.

You ought to likewise continue to assemble your portfolio. Utilize your investment benefits to expand your portfolio and buy more protections.

Strategy 3.
Stop Losses

Lara claims 100 Company Y stocks that she purchased at $600/share. Following a couple of months, the stock value rose to $800. This procured Lara a benefit of $2,000 ($8000 - $6000).

Lara felt that she could as of now unwind, so she went on a fourteen-day Caribbean voyage. She didn't check her record while still on a vacation. At the point when she returned from her get-away, she discovered that Company Y's stock value dropped to $400. She winds up losing a sum of $2,000.

To hold this back from happening to you, you should submit a breaking point or stop request with your broker to monitor your misfortunes. You can even put in a following stop request so you could determine the measure of misfortune you can endure.

You can stop your misfortunes physically on the off chance that you would prefer not to put in a stop request.

To do this, you need to screen the cost of your investments consistently. At the point when the cost of the stock starts to go down, put in a sell market request with your broker. To win reliably in the stock exchanging, you need to keep your misfortunes as low as could be expected.

Strategy 4.

Invest in a Company That Pays Dividends

Many "stock exchanging for novices" books will advise you to pick an organization that delivers profits. And that is solid counsel. As a general rule, profit installment means that an organization is doing extraordinary monetarily. Besides, it's a decent wellspring of normal pay, as well. Who would not like to get checks via the post office each quarter?

However, you should recollect that the organization can stop profit installments anytime. Organizations that deliver profits normally have a sluggish development rate since they are not reinvesting their benefits for extension.

Strategy 5.
Non-Correlated Assets

In the event that you need to turn into an effective investor, you don't just need to enhance your resources. It's additionally shrewd to invest in non-connected resources.

How about we take a gander at Tony's and Noel's story to show this point. They are both new investors and they chose to differentiate their portfolio and invest in various stocks.

Tony invested his cash in various informal communication organizations. Noel, then again, chose to take diversification to the following level. He invested in non-associated organizations. He invested a tad of his cash in tech organizations. Be that as it may, he likewise invested a tad in mining, food industry, and oil industry.

Following a couple of years, the informal communication industry eased back down and Tony wound up losing the vast majority of his cash. Noel additionally invested in long-range informal communication organizations; however he's actually doing extraordinary on the grounds that his investments are spread out across various businesses.

The technique for diversification is presumably quite possibly the main viewpoints in an investment plan. Diversification will assist you with receiving the rewards of investing in various territories and decline your danger. You need to pick investments that will perform diversely during various market conditions. For instance, on the off chance that you are anticipating expansion, at that point stocks that produce more pay will be advantageous during an inflationary period. On the off chance that you're anticipating resigning in 10 years, at that point development investments would be better right now.

On the off chance that you just have one kind of investment in your portfolio, (for example, all securities or all stocks), at that point it could seriously hurt your exhibition if there is a decline in that market. In the event that there was a financial slump and loan costs fell, being too intensely invested in bonds could mess genuine up for your portfolio.

Diversify your Portfolio to Minimize Risk and Maximize Gains

Diversification is key in managing an investment portfolio. Diverse investments spread out the risk and help protect against loss. A diverse mix of investments also helps maximize returns, since different asset classes tend to move independently of each other.

In the following chart we see how an investor's holdings are typically divided.

About 20% equities, 60% bonds, and 10% cash equivalents (either cash or a short-term fixed income investment). The remaining 10% should be in a mix of real estate or alternative investments such as gold or timber futures.

Each category has different risks associated with it. Below we will talk about the types of risk.

Security Risk

If you are the owner of a diversified portfolio, one way to reduce your security risk is to hold a broad mix of securities. This is because even if one sector in the market declines drastically, the other sectors may be performing well and thus generating income for you.

Exchange Rate Risk

If you invest your money outside of Canada, there is always exchange rate risk. That risk is that the value of your foreign holdings will drop because of the relative strength of the Canadian dollar compared to foreign currencies. In a diversified portfolio, some will benefit and some will suffer from this exchange rate risk.

Inflation Risk

Inflation is always a concern as prices rise over time. A diversified portfolio can help prevent inflation from eroding your income and capital, since different asset classes react differently to inflation. For example, equities tend to do well during periods when inflation rises. Bonds and cash holdings tend to lose value during periods of inflation.

Competition Risk

In order to increase market share and profits, employers often replace employees with newer technology or computers. Traditional investments such as bonds and cash equivalents may not always be able to compete with new technology for people's investment dollars. That means your money is at risk of being diverted into other types of investments.

Other Risks

Any type of investment can have unique risks associated with it. As time goes on, we face more and more challenges in trying to maintain a healthy financial portfolio. In order to do so, it's important that your investments include stocks from different sectors. This way, you're not betting everything on just one industry or company—and you can take advantage of opportunities outside of the U.S., which means more opportunity for growth! The next time you want to make an investment, diversify! You'll be glad you did when the economy takes a downturn. Having an appropriate portfolio management can assist you with remaining cold and increment your opportunity to make more benefit from investments with less danger than not doing anything by any stretch of the imagination. I will present a few methodologies for investors who are searching for ways to improve their portfolio management abilities and conquer passionate exchanging issue.

As everybody knows, not being passionate is vital in dealing with your investment. The market is always showing signs of change and sometimes it can go up or drop down in a brief timeframe. On the off chance that you are caught by dread, covetousness or frenzy, at that point you get no opportunity to make more benefit except for rather you will lose cash in spite of the fact that you have wise investments.

Thusly we ought to figure out how to control our feelings prior to exchanging for any investment. In any case it is difficult to make benefit regardless of whether we have great information about investment and exchanging strategies. Few individuals realize that traders can manage the feelings during investing measure by utilizing an appropriate technique called "investing brain science." Also, there are a few techniques which can be utilized to defeat the enthusiastic exchanging issue. As per Stock Charts, they referenced four stages for you. The first is to define your monetary goals and consider how much cash you might want to place into the investments. From that point forward, think about your capacity to bear hazard and figure out what sort of investment would be proper for you dependent on your danger resistance level. (Bear and buyer market may cause higher unpredictability in investment, yet it doesn't imply that high instability implies higher danger). Thirdly, choose how long you need to keep the investments and figure out what you would do if the market were to decay throughout a more drawn-out timeframe from your buy date. And finally, set up your investment hazard openness in rate terms, which will expect you to consider your age and target retirement date.

CHAPTER 13. PERSONAL ADVISOR AND ONLINE BROKERS

The internet has made many things easier, including the process of starting a personal budget. There are many resources available for advice on how to balance your income with your expenses. Personal advisers and online brokers offer different ways to stay on top of every dollar you spend, which is equally important for the personal investor and those looking to buy or sell real estate.

With so many websites out there, it might be hard to know where to start or what information you need in order to get started. We've compiled a list of some of the best sites that will allow you find your way from an initial budget plan, all the way up through retirement planning. By the end of this article, you should have a good idea of what your retirement budget should look like.

A great place to start is by setting a budget. While the initial step in creating a personal budget is deciding where every dollar goes, this isn't the only step in creating a plan that will help you reach your goals. Once you have figured out how much goes to every expense, it's time to create areas for savings and investment. Use this site to get started on plotting out your budget. Then use our recommended broker site as well as other websites for more detailed advice on how to invest wisely and create a comfortable retirement.

As a professional investor and general financial advisor, Suze Orman has helped thousands of people plan for their future with strategies for investing, saving, and avoiding debt. Her website provides an easy way for you to start running your own numbers to see how much money you will need to achieve your goals.

After determining how much goes to savings, where should that money go? Most people's first thought is to a savings account. Unfortunately, today's savings account can't provide the returns you need in order to reach your goals. If you're saving for retirement or college tuition, it's important that the funds are placed in an investment that grows at optimal rates. In order to do that, you need to invest in the stock market.

Robinhood is an investing app and brokerage that allows you to invest for free. It also provides all of the tools you could want in order to learn how to invest. This includes getting started guides on stock trading, research tools, educational resources, and even a financial news feed. They'll give you all of the information handouts you need to make informed decisions.

Once you've reviewed their app or signed up on their website, Robinhood will link up with your bank account for easy money transfers. Once the money is available, it's time to get started and start buying stocks. Once you have a portfolio started, it's time to make sure it's growing fast enough. Once you've been invested in the stock market for a certain period of time, it is important to look at your portfolio and see how much your stocks have grown. If they didn't perform as well as you hoped, what should you do? You have two main options. The first option is to sell your stocks and get a return on the current value of the stock. This may result in a small profit or loss, however. The second option is to re-balance your portfolio. This means that you take your current portfolio, and sell off the stocks that are doing worst. Then you move the money to the stocks that have done better, in order to bring everything back up to an even keel.

If your strategy is working well and your portfolio is growing, it's time to make some changes. The first thing you should do is look at how much risk you are taking with your investments. The riskier the investment, the higher potential there is for growth. However, these investments also hold much more risk of failure or loss. For example, the stock market as a whole is risky and could potentially crash.

What are personal advisers? Personal advisers are people who help answer your questions about investing, retirement planning, and other topics so that you can take control of your future. Fine-tuning these decisions may be as simple as choosing the right online brokerage or reading a few articles. That's where an online broker comes in handy.

The best personal advisers and online brokers don't just answer questions, but also help you to develop an investment strategy that's compatible with your risk tolerance and financial goals. For example, if you have a few million dollars sitting in an account, you may require a different investing strategy than someone with $50k. In this post, I will show exactly how to identify the best personal advisers and online brokers for your needs.

The first step is to figure out why you need a personal adviser or online broker in the first place. This is an important step because you can't always just compare the prices and terms of different personal advisers and online brokers for a certain service. For example, if you are looking to invest in cryptocurrencies, you will need a very different type of personal adviser or online broker than if you are thinking about buying stocks.

If you're looking for some great personal advice, check out a few online brokers and see what they offer. This can be a good way to compare rates, services, and policies before you sign on the dotted line. You can look at the benefits each of these companies offers before choosing which one is right for you. Online brokers are becoming more and more popular because it saves time and money—no need to drive around to different banks or wait in line! And just because it's convenient doesn't mean that it sacrifices quality or service—many online brokers offer free financial consultations with professional advisors who will gladly help you navigate life insurance options and investment strategies with ease. Once you have your account set up with an online broker, it's time to start looking into what kind of plan you need. Some of the options that you should consider include:

Term Life Insurance—This is actually one of the cheapest forms of life insurance that you can purchase, since it only covers for a certain amount of time (usually 20 years). The great thing about this policy is that it will never become outdated like permanent policies do, so even if you don't need protection after the first twenty years, the policy will still be good in case you need coverage at a later date.

Universal Life—This type of insurance plan provides multiple options for death benefits along with flexible premium payment plans and low rates.

Term Universal Life—This is one of the most popular types of universal life policies. The policy covers your family for a specified amount of time (i.e., 30 years) and can be financed over that time period.

How to Open a Broker Account

Opening a broker account can be daunting, especially for a beginner. Beginners may not know what to expect and may feel bombarded by the myriad of options and possibilities when looking at different accounts.

What types of brokerage accounts are there?

- Regular Brokerage Account: This type of brokerage account typically has high trading fees and minimum payment requirements. These types of brokerage accounts don't come with any financial advice or guidance unless you pay for it separately.

- Discount Brokerage Account: A discount brokerage account has lower trading fees and offers more services than regular brokerage accounts. Discount brokerages usually provide financial advice as well as guidance on how to invest your money.

How can I tell the difference between a good and a bad broker?

Look at their historical performance chart. The best brokers will have the most recent performance data available, which should be displayed on their website. The data will show how well they have performed over time, as well as what kind of fees they charge for each kind of transaction you might make through them (trading fees, account maintenance fees etc.). Look at the minimum requirements for starting an account—some brokers might require larger amounts than others. Call up the broker and ask about their services. It's best if you can speak with a real person to get a feeling of how helpful they are and what kind of customer service they provide.

What should I be looking for when opening an account?

A good broker will display all available information on their website so you can easily decide whether or not it's the right broker for you. Look at the financial health of the brokerage firm—this is usually displayed on their website as well. You should look at whether or not they are a member of any regulatory bodies, like the SEC or FINRA. If they are a member of such bodies, it means that they have undergone a certain level of scrutiny by the institution. You can also look up their latest financial reports with the SEC.

Can I open an account without depositing any money?

Some discount brokerages will allow you to open an account without depositing any money—though some might require a little bit of collateral in order to provide you with the initial trading/investing tools (like a working phone number and email address). It's best if you can fill out your profile completely before applying for an account—don't leave any fields blank! This way, when you apply for an account, there will be less information required from you.

How do I fund my account?

You can fund your account by depositing money, via a wire transfer or by using a credit/debit card. Be sure to look at the deposit and withdrawal requirements for each type of funding method so you can make your payment in a timely manner.

What is the minimum amount required to open an account?

Different brokers have different requirements for opening an account—some require more than others. You'll want to look at the minimum funding requirements for the broker so that you can have enough money on hand when you make your initial deposit. If the amount is too high, you may have to get financing from a third party.

What are some of the pros and cons of opening a brokerage account?

The most important thing to keep in mind when deciding if opening a brokerage account is right for you, is whether or not you will be able to follow through with it. It's best to find out as much information as possible about these accounts before actually applying for one. Once you have all of the facts straight, you can decide whether or not opening a brokerage account is right for you!

Can they open the various accounts themselves or do they need a parent or guardian to do so?

Yes, your teen can open an account on his or her own.

Do they need a parent or guardian to add money to the account?

Yes. In order for the account to be funded, at least one of our members must act as a co-owner/co-applicant to the account and deposit funds into the joint brokerage account. This is because we check if there are no sanctions against trading, that means, if you have no criminal record in any country. Also, we check if you are not registered in any other brokers from which we receive reports that you trade with them. And only after all these checks is done, we accept customers to our company and fund their accounts.

Are there any limitations or facilities for teenagers who put away and/or invest small amounts?

Yes, there is a facility for teens to open a trading account. The account can be opened either in the name of the child or parent. Brokerage will be charged for interest credited on such accounts and/or other financial benefits.

CHAPTER 14. BEST INVESTING AND MICRO-SAVINGS APPS

Finding extra money to invest is often a challenge. The accounts offered by traditional banks are appealing because they require no deposit or minimum balance, but the rates are generally low and the fees can be high. Fortunately, there are apps that will help you make it much easier to invest and save more money—without the headaches of old-fashioned banking. This details some of those app options for investing and saving, along with what each of their strengths and weaknesses may be. These apps offer features like intuitive interfaces, automatic deposits, tax-free growth in states with low-income taxes or none at all, and debit cards for easy access to your funds. Hopefully this information will help you find a savings account that fits your goals and needs.

1) Acorns

Acorns is an investing app for people who want to start small in their investing adventures. What makes it different from other apps is that Acorns uses a round-up system to invest your money for you. That means you can invest any amount of money, even if it's just $0.25 left at the end of the day after coffee or something. All you have to do is link a debit card to the app and when you use it, Acorns rounds up any purchases over $1 and invests the difference into exchange-traded funds (ETFs). The Acorns app is available on both iOS and Android, and it's a great option for those who don't want to worry about how much money needs to be invested or where the investments are being made. Plus, it allows you to connect with friends to reach your goals faster. While Acorns is definitely one of the best investing apps out there, it isn't the best micro-saving option. The round-up system can sometimes take a while to get going when you're only investing $0.25 here and there. But if you have more than enough money to invest, then this might be a great way to do it without worrying about anything else but putting your money into investments that will grow over time.

2) Robinhood

Robinhood is a financial app that lets you invest in stocks and ETFs for free with no hidden fees. The app, which is currently only available on Android and iOS, also allows you to buy and sell stock for just $0 commission. All you have to do is sign up with your name, email address and phone number, connect your bank account or credit card (you can also connect a brokerage if you want), link your bank account or credit card, choose how much of your deposit goes into savings versus investments, and that's it. Your money will be in the market within minutes. The next step is choosing stocks or other investment options. It's relatively easy to browse through the available options and see which ones seem like good investments. The app provides a specific set of alerts that will let you know when you have made money in your investments, and it also lets you view your actual account (how much money is in it, how much interest has been earned on the deposits, how many stocks are being held in the portfolio).

While Robinhood definitely comes with its own set of advantages, there are some drawbacks. For one thing, it does not support automatic deposits like Acorns does. Plus it doesn't support micro-investing or tax-free withdrawals because of its status as an investment app. Also, it's not much of a micro-saving app because there is no option for automatic deposits. Overall, however, it's pretty high on our list of the best investing and micro-savings apps.

3) Qapital

Qapital is an app that works as both a micro-saving and investing tool. It automatically transfers money from your checking account to a "virtual" savings account linked to the app and then invests that money in various ways. It offers easy access to checking and debit card functions when you need them, and it also supports automated payment options such as recurring monthly bills or paying yourself first for savings goals.

Qapital is a great option for micro-savings because it adds up your total savings amount over time and determines how much you should save. It's also a great investing app because it rounds up purchases when you use your debit card and invests the difference into one of its five investment categories: bank transfers, mutual funds, stocks, crowdfunding and charity.

Qapital is also host to more than just investing tools. The app also offers automated rules that will remind you to pay yourself first or save for something special. This makes it easy to manage your budget on a day-to-day basis while also saving money on things like recurring monthly bills. The Qapital app can be downloaded for free from the App Store and Google Play.

4) Acorns Spend

Acorns Spend is a feature that was added to the Acorns app in 2017. It's geared mainly toward people who want to save money for something special, like a wedding or a vacation, rather than simply invest money. It allows you to set savings goals, track your progress toward those goals, and set up automatic deposits so you can continue saving without having to worry about it too much or having to think about where your money is going. Plus, you get access to a debit card for quick access or payments wherever you need them.

Unlike Acorns Invest, you have to pay a monthly fee of $1.00 for the privilege of using Acorns Spend, but that fee is waived if you are a student or if you have an investment account with Acorns.

5) CapitalOne Investing

CapitalOne Investing is another one of the great options for do-it-yourself investors who want to choose their own investments and personalize each investment strategy for their specific goals. CapitalOne Investing allows you to choose from over 6,000 exchange-traded funds (ETFs), stocks, mutual funds and bonds available in its portfolio.

You can choose to invest automatically or manually, and you have free access to funds from your bank account. If you need help, however, CapitalOne Investing offers resources such as investment guidance and community forums so that you can get advice whenever you need it.

The Best Investing Apps

If you're an investor with no access to a financial advisor, but who still want to be in the market, these apps can help. They are all designed for people looking for a simpler, more hands-off way to invest and each offers different advantages. These are the best investing apps we've found.

These days, it seems like every app claims they can help you make more money with your investments. But can they? And are these apps really the best way to invest in your long-term financial goals? If you're a DIY investor with no access to a financial advisor, then of course, we recommend that you try to time the market. Seriously. You most certainly should.

But if you've tried and failed—and we know many of you have—then there are much better ways to make the most out of the money in your 401(k) than trying to time the market. These "best-investing apps" are designed for people looking for a simpler, more hands-off way of investing.

We review five options. Each offers a different advantage, and all you have to do is decide which best fits your needs.

Google's Smart Banking App

When Google unveiled its new smart banking app in July, the big selling point was multiple logins. That's the feature that set it apart from Apple's similar offering, which only works on the iPhone for now. But don't overlook the other perks—like ATM finder, balance alerts and even a budget-management tab where you can review your spending trends. The Google Product Manager of Financial Services, Jonathan Alferness, told us it was designed for people looking to manage their bank accounts from anywhere. *"It's not specifically designed for high-net-worth investors,"* he said. *"It's designed for anyone who has bank accounts and wants access to them from anywhere."*

The Google Smart Banking App also provides market data to help you stay on top of the market with free real-time quotes and access to your latest account information whenever you want it—even when you aren't online.

Of course, the app can also send you alerts when your bank account balance falls to a certain level, or if there's an unusual transaction. The Smart Banking App is available for users of Bank of America, American Express, Capital One, Discover, HSBC, Navy Federal Credit Union and U.S. Bank. For now, it's mostly geared towards people with checking accounts—but Google will soon also offer savings-account and credit-card functions via the app as well. If you have a busy life—one that doesn't leave you with tons of time to monitor your investments on a minute-by-minute basis—then this may be the best investing app for you.

Fidelity Investments' Fidelity Go App

If you're looking to manage your investments from a smartphone or iPad, the Fidelity Go app is another smart choice. The interface is clean and intuitive—and it allows you to access your accounts on the go. Using the app, you can record your investment transactions, check up on their value any time of day and manage your cash flow from any location.

Fidelity also provides you with real-time quotes and charts, so you can stay on top of the market. And it's free to use.

If you're an investor with a number of different accounts, try to keep things simple by consolidating them all into a Fidelity account. Then just check the balances—and their progress—using the app. You won't have to worry about monitoring multiple accounts, or logging in and out of several different ones.

The Fidelity Go app is available for iPhone users. It works with any brokerage or retirement account at Citi, Morgan Stanley, JP Morgan or other firms that connect to Fidelity.

Acorns' Investing App

Acorns take the stock market out of individual investors' hands using its "spare change" investing app. It was designed so you can invest money in open-end mutual funds and real-estate investment trusts (REITs) through the app. All you do is connect your debit card to a FOLIOfn account and then set up a recurring purchase—every week, for example—for pennies at a time. Over time those small amounts have added up to some pretty impressive returns for many investors, including an annualized return of 8% over the last five years—with no account minimum. And if you want to begin investing, you don't have to set up an account or make an initial deposit. Just link your debit card. The app will automatically round up every purchase you make by a certain amount—typically a dollar or two—and put that money into one of five investment portfolios. The amount it rounds up is added to your investments but deducted from your balance. So, it doesn't cost you anything extra in fees. It's like having someone else investing for you so that one day when you find yourself financially secure, you can give back to others who aren't as fortunate as you are now.

Conclusion

The basic idea behind stock investing is pretty simple: to buy a share of a company you believe will perform well in the future. This means that the company needs to have a strong business or product, and it needs to be led by strong leadership. When a company performs well, and the stock is purchased at a lower price, you can sell the stock for more than you paid. This means that if your stock performs well over time, you make money.

The nice thing about owning stocks is that once they are bought, there's not much else to worry about: dividends will be paid out occasionally by the company, but that's not your concern; all you have to do is track whether or not your investment increases or decreases in value over time.

Sounds easy, right? Unfortunately, it's not quite so simple. One of the most frustrating things about investing in stocks is that it isn't always obvious what a company's share is worth. This is what we mean when we talk about a company's value (or stock price). The value of a company is constantly changing, giving investors headaches and making it hard to decide if they want to invest in this stock or that.

Is Investing in Stocks a Good Idea?

There's no one correct answer to this question. Some people are successful at investing and make a lot of money. In contrast, others lose out and don't get anything from their investment. Remember, a stock is only worth what someone else is willing to pay for it. If you have no idea how the stock market works or how much a company is worth, you can lose a lot of money.

So be smart about where you invest your money! If you're interested in buying stocks, you should do as much research as possible before making any investment. That means reading as many books and articles about investing as possible. It also means taking a class on investing if your school offers one. There are many different investing methods and approaches. When you start any new activity, you have to learn the rules to enable you to play the game in the best way. No matter how exciting the stock market appears, there is a certain amount of history involved. There are several popular ways to invest or trade stocks, but they all involve some high-risk potential. The first step in understanding the world of stock investment is to ensure that you receive a solid education on what both sides mean by terms such as "investing" and "trading".

To trade stocks means to buy them and sell them within a short period. The most famous example of this is when traders are in an unstable market. These investors use the stock market as a short-term replacement for income, essentially gambling that they can make more money within a brief period than it would cost to invest in the shares. The rule here is that the faster you sell your stock, the higher you will profit. The longer you wait to sell your investment, however, the more likely you are to lose out on potential gains.

Investing, on the other hand, is a far less risky method. In this instance, the investor profits from the company's growth over time. Investing in stocks is a longer-term strategy used to make money over several years or even decades. You can use the stock market to get some of the advantages of earning an income. When you invest in stocks, you are getting multiple cash over the years, with relatively little risk to your portfolio or your financial future.

The best way to be successful at stock investing is to keep in mind that it is only as risky as you allow it to be. If you put your money in safe investments such as government bonds and CDs, then your capital will not grow very much. This means that when you retire, you will not have much money left over. Suppose you want to make your money work for you and increase your capital. In that case, you need to put it in investment situations that are likely to increase in value over time.

Many stock investments will never go up in value. This is why it is essential to get the most reliable information available when you invest your money. One of the best ways to get information, and avoid scams, is to talk to someone who knows what they are doing.

The bottom line here is that there are several ways that you can invest your money for the future, but it always comes down to common sense and sound research. Don't ever rush into anything, and always verify that the investment is worthwhile. The sooner you start investing in your future, the better. Many people miss out on significant opportunities because they fail to take advantage of every opportunity that comes their way, and the stock market is a great place to make some cash. In order to get the best possible results, though, make sure that you educate yourself first.

We've talked in this guide about compound interest. The compound interest (also called "compound interest") is an amount of money that has been multiplied by the interest rate over time.

For example, if a person received 10 dollars from their bank account, and then the bank gave the person 5 % of interest on it, their new amount would be 11.50 dollars. The original amount of money is called the principal. Then, the amount of money after being invested is called compound interest.

On the other hand, investing at a young age brings many benefits:

1. **You will have a significant investment tool choice since you have more time to invest and gather more knowledge about how to make money by investing.** The reason for this is simple, when you are in your 40's or 50's, you will be focused on saving for retirement, your kid's education, or other things like buying a house or purchasing a car, and thus it will be much harder to learn about how to make money by investing and thus harder to save enough money for those goals.

2. **It will give you a head start in our global financial system**. Many of the people who become millionaires are simply the ones who started investing early, this is especially true in China since in our country there are many poor families that struggle to pay for their children's education and if you become rich earlier, it will be a lot easier to have your kids study abroad or attend an expensive private school.

3. **It will give you the power to make large investments.** If you are a young man or woman who is already making decent money, it will be much easier for you to make large stock and real estate investments. There is no doubt that making a single investment of $10,000 is a lot easier than saving up this amount of money while having bills to pay at the same time.

4. **It will be easier for you to accumulate wealth since investing** in your 20's means that you have many years ahead of you to keep investing more, so even if your rate of return is just 10%, it can still turn into a considerable amount when invested year after year.

5. **It will help you build a network of friends who are wealthy and who will be able to help you get opportunities in life**. You might have a friend who already run his own successful company or is already a successful businessman, if so then this will

greatly improve your chances of getting a job that pays you comfortably.

6. **Finally, you should always have a plan B for what to do if things go wrong**. If you're reading this, then that means that you're really interested in making money by investing and making smart choices with your investments.

www.ingramcontent.com/pod-product-compliance
Lightning Source LLC
LaVergne TN
LVHW080530210926
848481LV00019B/811
9781807651060